Adventures in Art

Laura H. Chapman

Davis Publications, Inc.

Worcester, Massachusetts

Front cover: *Student artwork by Holly Dyer, Bethel-Tate School, Bethel, Ohio. From the Crayola® Dream-Makers® Collection, courtesy of Binney & Smith Inc.*

Title page: *Claude Monet, Poppy Field in a Hollow Near Giverny, 1885. Oil on canvas, 25 5/8 x 32" (65 x 81 cm). The Museum of Fine Arts, Boston (Juliana Cheney Edwards Collection; bequest of Robert J. Edwards in memory of his mother).*

Editorial Advisory Board:

Dr. Cynthia Colbert
Professor of Art
and Chair of Art Education
University of South Carolina
Columbia, South Carolina

Bill MacDonald
Art Education Consultant
Vancouver, British Columbia
Canada

Dr. Connie Newton
Assistant Professor of Art
School of Visual Art
University of North Texas
Denton, Texas

Sandra Noble
Curriculum Specialist for the Fine Arts
Cleveland Public Schools
Cleveland, Ohio

Reading Consultant:

Dr. JoAnn Canales
College of Art Education
University of North Texas
Denton, Texas

Reviewers:

Cliff Cousins
Art Specialist
Davenport Community School District–
Davenport, Iowa

Dr. Lila G. Crespin
College of Fine Art
California State University at
Long Beach

Lee Gage
Art Supervisor
Westchester Area School District
Westchester, Pennsylvania

William Gay, Jr.
Visual Art Coordinator
Richland County School District One
Columbia, South Carolina

Dr. Adrienne W. Hoard
Associate Professor
University of Missouri-Columbia

Mary Jordan
Visual Arts Curriculum Specialist
Tempe, Arizona

Kathleen Lockhart
Curriculum & Instructional Specialist
Baltimore, Maryland

David McIntyre
Consultant for Visual Arts
El Paso Independent School District
El Paso, Texas

R. Barry Shauck
Supervisor of Art
Howard County Public School
Ellicott City, Maryland

Linda Sleight
Visual Arts Curriculum Specialist
Tempe, Arizona

Carl Yochum
Director of Fine Arts
Ferguson-Florissant School District
Florissant, Missouri

Joyce Young
Assistant Principal
Bond Hill School
Cincinnati, Ohio

Acknowledgements:
The author and publisher would like to thank the following individuals and groups for their special assistance in providing images, resources and other help: Tom Feelings, Mickey Ford, Claire Mowbray Golding, Colleen Kelley, Samella Lewis, Maya Nigrosh, Sandra Palmer, Dawn Reddy, Tara Reddy, Patricia A. Renick, Chloë Sayer, Martha Siegel, Martin Speed, Bernice Steinbaum, Anne Straus, and art teachers in the Department of Defense Dependent Schools.

Managing Editor:
Wyatt Wade

Editor:
Laura J. Marshall

Design:
Douglass Scott, WGBH Design

Production:
Nancy Dutting

Photo Acquisitions:
Allan Harper

Illustrator:
Susan Christy-Pallo

Photography:
Schlowsky Photography

Contents

Page

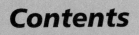

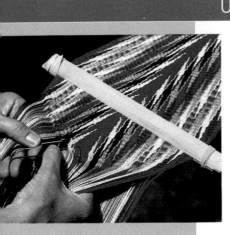

What is Art
Seeing and Creating Art

B Finger weaving. Photograph: Veronique Deplanne.

A **Sunset, Newport Beach, California.** Photograph: Woody Woodworth, Superstock, Inc.

You can think about **art** in many ways. Many people say art is something very beautiful in nature, like a rainbow or a sunset. Do you think the sunset in picture A is art? Why or why not?

Some people say that art is a carefully made object, like a woven cloth. Are the weavings in pictures B and C done with great skill? Are the designs carefully planned? Do you think the weavings are art?

There are other ways to think about art. Art is a way to share what you see and feel. You can create artworks that tell stories. You can draw pictures or model clay to express your ideas.

Finished finger weaving (detail). Photograph: Veronique Deplanne.

D Photograph: Dorothy Johnson.

In this unit you will learn how artists see their world. The special things artists see are called the **elements of design**. Some of the elements are line, color and shape. Others are texture, form and space.

Artists also plan their artwork. Artists plan the way colors and shapes fit together in a design. In this unit, you will learn how artists make plans by using **principles of design.** A principle is a guide for thinking about an artwork's design.

Sketching
Drawing People Who Pose

Rosa Bonheur, *Studies of a Fawn.* Oil on paper, mounted to canvas, 15 x 20 3/4" (38 x 53 cm). The Snite Museum of Art, University of Notre Dame, Indiana (On extended loan from Mr. & Mrs. Noah L. Butkin).

Have you ever wondered how artists get ideas for their work? One way is by making sketches. **Sketches** are drawings you make to learn things. A sketch can help you remember what you see.

Do you like to make sketches?

What are some of your favorite things to draw?

Look at the sketches in picture A. The artist loved to study animals. She made sketches to learn how animals look and move around. Why do you think she sketched so many views of a fawn?

 Jean-François Millet, *The Gleaners,* 1857. Black conte crayon on off-white china paper, 6 7/8 x 10 3/8" (17 x 26 cm). The George A. Lucas Collection of The Maryland Institute, College of Art, on indefinite loan to the Baltimore Museum of Art.

D Student artwork.

C **Jean-François Millet,** *The Gleaners,* 1857. Oil on canvas, 18 1/4 x 24" (46 x 61 cm). Musée de Orsay, Paris. © Photo R.M.N.

Sometimes artists make sketches to **design**, or plan, an artwork. The sketch in picture B was made with black crayon. The artist made the sketch to plan his painting in picture C. How are the sketch and the painting alike? How are they different?

A student made the sketch in picture D. She drew a classmate who was wearing a costume. Have you ever sketched a model? Have you ever taken a **pose** so someone could sketch you?

Lines and Shapes
Drawing Imaginary Places

A   **Alexander Calder, *Autumn Leaves,*** 1971. Tapestry, woven by Pinton Freres. By Courtesy of the Trustees of the Crown Copyright. Victoria and Albert Museum, London.

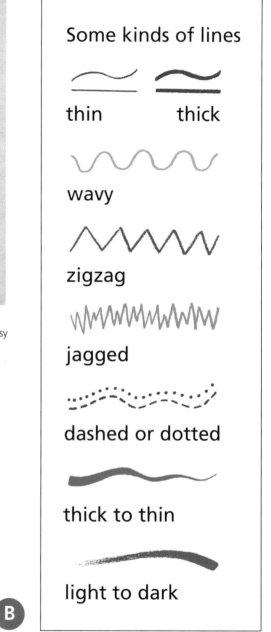

Some kinds of lines

thin   thick

wavy

zigzag

jagged

dashed or dotted

thick to thin

light to dark

B

Look at the lines and shapes in picture A. Alexander Calder created looping **lines** and curved **shapes** in this artwork. Why do the lines and shapes go with the title of his artwork?

Look at the lines in picture B. When might you want to draw thin or thick lines? wavy or zigzag lines? Can you think of other kinds of lines? What ideas or feelings might go with the lines?

What art materials do you like to use for drawing? Do pencil lines look the same as lines made with a marker or crayon? What other **media** can you use to create lines?

Joan Miró, *The Hermitage,* 1924. Oil and/or aqueous medium, crayon and pencil, 45 x 57 7/8" (114 x 147 cm). Philadelphia Museum of Art (The Louise & Walter Arensberg Collection).

C

Can you find shapes like these?

D

Joan Miró liked to create artworks about make-believe places, animals and people. His painting in picture C has dotted lines and wavy lines. Do you see zigzag lines? What other lines do you see?

When lines meet or cross each other they make a shape. What shapes do you see in pictures A and C? Do some shapes remind you of things you know about? Why?

Alexander Calder and Joan Miró created **imaginative** artwork. An imaginative artwork is one you make up. It is not meant to look realistic.

Draw a picture of a make-believe place. Use your imagination. The place you draw could be strange or beautiful. Funny or dream-like things could happen there. What lines and shapes will you use for your artwork?

11

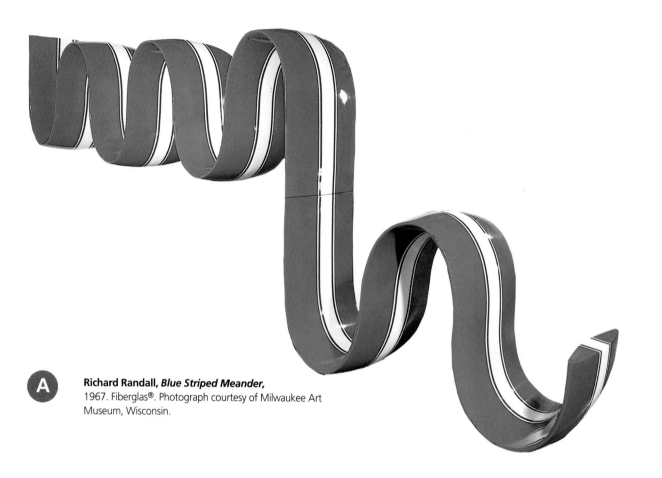

A **Richard Randall, *Blue Striped Meander*,** 1967. Fiberglas®. Photograph courtesy of Milwaukee Art Museum, Wisconsin.

Artists create sculptures, paintings and other kinds of art. Sometimes they use lines to express ideas or feelings about **motion**.

The sculpture in picture A is a ribbon-like line in space. Pretend you can move your hand across the sculpture. What kind of motion do you feel?

The photograph in picture B is a record of motion. The photograph shows cars moving on a highway. Why do the lines help you see the motion?

B **Garden State Parkway, New Jersey.** Photograph: Scott McKiernan. © 1993 Scott McKiernan.

Look at the colorful lines and shapes in picture C. Some of the lines are wavy or wiggly. Some of the lines loop or zigzag. Why do these lines create a feeling of motion? What else did the artist want you to see?

Practice drawing lines that show motion. What lines might show the motion of a jet plane? a jazzy dance? a grasshopper? a snake?

After you practice, draw a picture filled with "action" lines. You might repeat one action line many times. You might draw a variety of action lines.

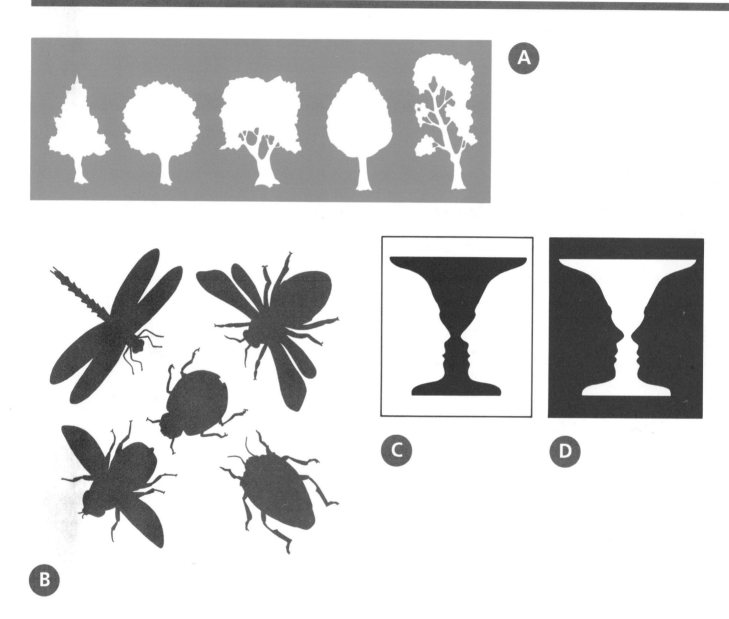

Almost everything you see has one main shape. Look at the trees in picture A. Can you name the main shapes? How are the main shapes in picture B alike? How are they different?

In art, the first shapes you see are called **positive shapes**. The background shapes are called **negative shapes**.

The negative shapes in an artwork can be just as important as the positive shapes. Look at pictures C and D. Find the vase in both of them. Can you also see two faces? Why?

 M.C. Escher, *Sky and Water I*, 1938. Woodcut, 17 3/8 x 17 3/8" (44 x 44 cm). Collection Haags Gemeentemuseum, the Hague.

Artists plan the positive and negative shapes in their artwork. Sometimes the main and background shapes are like parts of a puzzle. Can you find the positive and negative shapes in picture E?

Cut some positive shapes from paper. Save all of your background or negative shapes. You will use all your shapes in the next lesson.

You can make a stencil print. A **stencil** is made by cutting a positive shape from stiff paper. The stiff paper with the hole is your stencil. It can be used many times for printing.

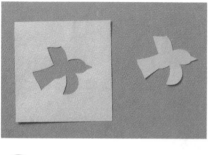

 A

You can print a stencil with paint and a sponge. Gently press down on the sponge. Do you see how the paint should look?

Stencils can be used to print on paper or cloth. The traffic arrows on roads are made with large stencils. Where else have you seen stencil printing?

 C

B

 Student artwork.

Stencils can help you make a picture with repeated shapes. You can make stencil prints with paint, chalk or crayons.

You can combine stencils to make a picture. Four children used stencils to make picture D. What parts of the picture did they print first? Why do you think so? They also printed negative shapes. Do you know how?

E

Balance and Rhythms
A Collage

A **Henri Matisse, *Large Composition With Masks,*** 1953. Paper on canvas (collage), 139 1/4 x 392 1/2" (354 x 997 cm).
© 1992 National Gallery of Art, Washington, DC (Ailsa Mellon Bruce Fund).

Have you ever created a collage? A **collage** is a picture made from paper shapes. Henri Matisse created this large collage.

Henri Matisse liked to cut paper without drawing the shapes first. He cut out many shapes for each collage. He tried different ways to arrange shapes. When he liked a design, he pasted the shapes down.

Many of the shapes in this collage are identical, or exactly alike. Can you find some of them? Can you find shapes that are similar but not identical?

This collage has symmetry. **Symmetry** means that the left and right sides of the design are alike, or equally balanced.

This collage also has visual rhythms. **Visual rhythms** are planned by repeating shapes, colors and spaces. How are visual rhythms like rhythms in dance or music?

Make a collage. Plan a design that has symmetry and visual rhythms. Learn to cut identical shapes from thin paper.

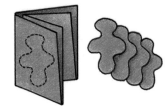

B Fold one paper twice.

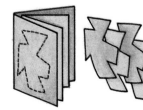

Fold two papers once.

Texture
See and Touch Textures

Max Ernst, *Whip Lashes or Lava Threads,* ca. 1925. Pencil frottage on off-white wove paper, 10 1/4 x 16 11/16" (26 x 42 cm). The Baltimore Museum of Art (Gift of Mme. Helena Rubenstein).

Textures can be rough or smooth, bumpy or silky. You can feel textures by touching objects. You can see textures by making a **rubbing**. To make a rubbing, put paper over a surface that has bumps or grooves. Hold the paper still. Rub the paper with the flat side of a pencil point, crayon or oil pastel.

Max Ernst's rubbing, in picture A, shows the texture of pieces of thread. He said the lines looked like lava flowing from a volcano. What other textures do you see in his rubbing?

Artist Eva Ruiz created the artwork in picture B. It is a collage made from rubbings of a floor. She taped paper to the floor. She rubbed the paper with two colors of crayon.

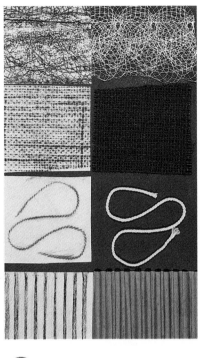

B | Eva Ruiz, *Memories of Home*, 1992. Crayon rubbing, 8 1/2 x 10" (22 x 25 cm). Courtesy of the artist.

C | Student artwork.

Eva Ruiz brushed watery paint on her best rubbings. The paint rolled away from the wax crayon. This process is called **crayon resist**. When the paint dried, she made the collage.

A student created the artwork in picture C. He collected scraps of cloth, string and textured paper.

Then he made rubbings. His rubbings show the visual textures. The objects he glued down have tactile textures. **Tactile** means a texture you know by using your sense of touch.

8

Invented Textures
Drawing Animals

 Rembrandt van Rijn, *Hog* (detail), 1643. Etching, 5 5/8 x 6" (14 x 15 cm). Reproduced by Courtesy of the Trustees of the British Museum, London.

Have you ever seen or touched the textures of a real hog? Look at picture A. Does the texture of this hog look rough or smooth? silky or prickly? What lines help you see the texture?

Sometimes artists use lines to show textures and **patterns**. Look at the cat in picture B. The striped pattern has many thin lines in rows. The thin lines also remind you of the texture of fur. What animals have you seen with patterns and textures?

 Unknown, *Cat,* Engraving from the book *Russkiia Narodnyia Kartink* by Dmitrii Alexandrovich Rovinskii, 1881-1893. Engraving. Collection, Ryerson Library. © 1992, The Art Institute of Chicago. All Rights Reserved.

The drawing in picture C shows the spiky texture of a porcupine. What lines create the feeling of a rough texture?

Think of a real or imaginary animal to draw. Experiment with different ways to draw the textures and patterns of the animal. Use a pencil, marker or crayon. You might combine some of these drawing **media**. When you make your drawing, use what you learned from your experiments.

A   **Linda Lomahaftewa,** *Animal Prayer Offering,* 1988. Monoprint, 22 x 30″ (56 x 76 cm). Courtesy of the artist.

A North American Indian artist created the artwork in picture A. The artist's ancestors are Hopi and Choctaw Indians. Her ancestors taught her to respect nature. The animal-like **symbol** stands for the spirit of many animals. The background suggests the motion of wind and stars in the sky.

This artwork is a **monoprint**. Mono- means one. The artist made only one print like this one.

A monoprint is made by following several steps. First you put ink or paint on a smooth sheet of metal or plastic. Then you wipe away some of the ink or paint to create lines and textures.

B Student artwork.

1. Create your design in wet paint or ink.

2. Place paper over the design. Rub it all over.

3. Lift the paper. This is called pulling the print.

While the ink or paint is wet, put a full sheet of paper over the whole design. Rub the whole paper to press the ink or paint onto it.

A student made the monoprint in picture B. He used a cotton swab to create lines for the fence and grass. He placed the paper shapes on top of the wet ink. What did he do next? Why?

10

Plans for Patterns
Print a Clay Stamp

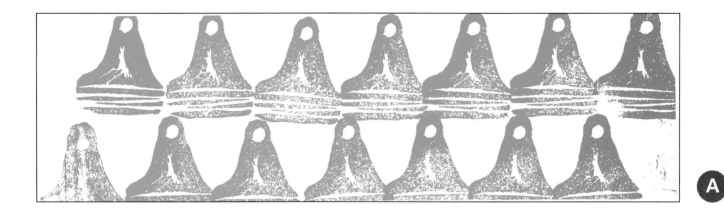

A

Artists plan patterns for fabrics, wallpaper and other flat **surfaces**. Look around your room for patterns. How can you tell if the designs make a pattern?

Printing is one way to **repeat** a design and create a pattern. The designs in this lesson were made with printing stamps.

An artist printed these designs on paper. She made the printing stamp from clay.

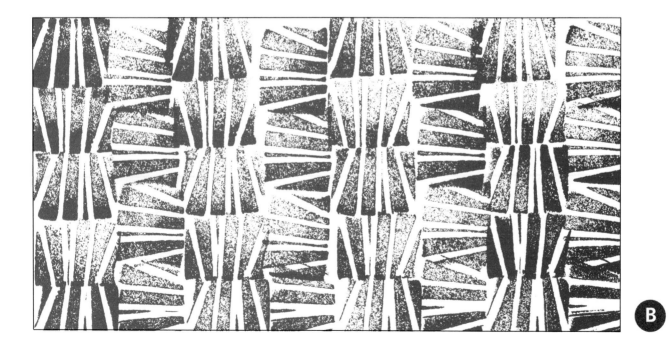

B

C

Look at the design in picture B. Imagine you were printing it with the stamp in picture C. How could you print the stamp in even rows? Could you create other patterns from the same stamp? How?

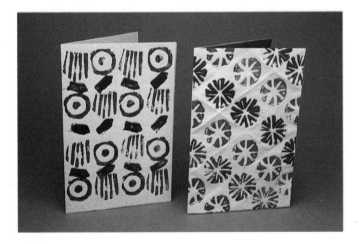

D Student artwork.

Students made printing stamps from clay. They made covers for booklets. You can make and print a clay stamp.

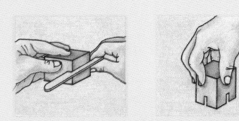

1. Press a design in clay. Make deep grooves in a flat surface.

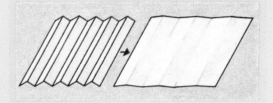

2. Fold paper, then flatten. Use the folds to plan a pattern.

3. Press your stamp on a pad, then print it.

 A   **William Doriani, *Flag Day,*** 1935. Oil on canvas, 12 1/4 x 35 5/8" (31 x 98 cm). Collection, The Museum of Modern Art, New York (The Sidney and Harriet Janis Collection).

Can you see the **visual rhythms** in this painting? Look for the repeated lines, colors and shapes. The repeated elements make a pattern. The pattern helps you to see the rhythm of the march.

Do you see how shapes of people in the first row overlap other shapes? **Overlap** means that some shapes are in front of other shapes. How do the shapes create a rhythm?

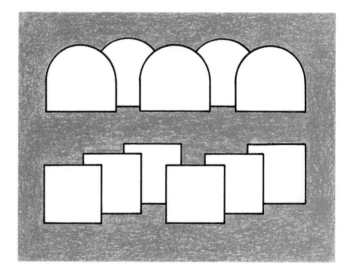

B

An artist created the painting in picture C. Which shapes overlap? Can you find some visual rhythms?

Create a picture of many people, animals, cars or buildings. Overlap some of the shapes. Repeat some lines, colors and shapes to create a visual rhythm.

 José Clemente Orozco, _Zapatistas,_ 1931. Oil on canvas, 45 x 55" (114 x 140 cm). Collection, The Museum of Modern Art, New York (Given anonymously).

 Anne Leone, *Water Series XI*, 1988. Oil on linen, 24 x 30" (48 x 76 cm).
Private Collection, London, England. Courtesy of the artist.

What **hues**, or colors, do you see in this painting? Artists say hues are related, like members of a family. Most of the hues in this painting are **cool colors**.

Cool colors are blue, green and violet. **Related** cool **colors** are yellow-green, blue-green and blue-violet. Why are these colors called "cool?" How are the colors related?

Why did this artist use cool colors in her painting? Do you think the artist painted exactly what she saw?

Emil Nolde, *Still Life, Tulips,* ca. 1930. Watercolor on paper, 18 1/2 x 13 1/2"
(47 x 34 cm). North Carolina Museum of Art, Raleigh (Bequest of W. R. Valentiner).

Most of the colors in this painting are warm hues. Warm colors are red, yellow and orange. Related warm colors are yellow-orange, red-orange and red-violet.

Many artists plan artworks around a "family" of related colors. You have learned about two families of colors: cool and warm.

A color family helps to give unity to an artwork. **Unity** means that things go together. Each painting is unified by using a family of related colors.

31

 Claude Monet, *Poppy Field in a Hollow Near Giverny,* 1885. Oil on canvas, 25 5/8 x 32" (65 x 81 cm). The Museum of Fine Arts, Boston (Juliana Cheney Edwards Collection. Bequest of Robert J. Edwards in memory of his mother).

Many artists love to create paintings of colorful scenes. Claude Monet liked to see color and light outdoors. Why do you think he wanted to paint this scene?

You can create colorful paintings. You can mix many colors from just three colors: red, yellow and blue. These three colors are called **primary colors**.

Orange, green and violet are called **secondary colors**. Look at the color wheel in picture B. What secondary color do you get by mixing yellow and red? How can you mix green? Violet?

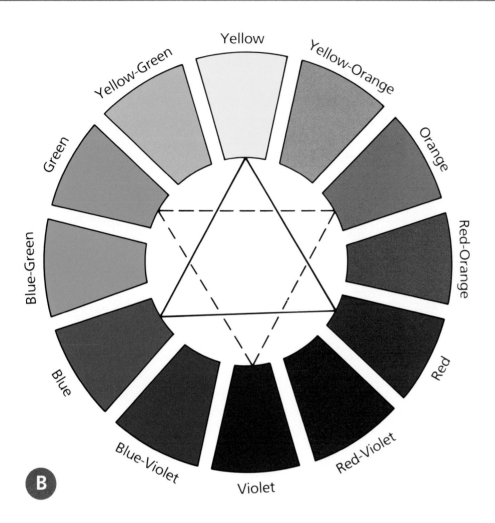

Yellow

Yellow-Green

Yellow-Orange

Green

Orange

Blue-Green

Red-Orange

Blue

Red

Blue-Violet

Red-Violet

Violet

B

1. Begin with a primary color.

2. Add a "dot" of another primary color.

3. Mix the two colors together.

Practice mixing secondary colors. Then mix some **intermediate colors** such as yellow-orange and yellow-green. Can you find some intermediate colors in pictures A and B? How can you mix intermediate colors?

After you practice mixing colors, paint a colorful picture. You might show a blazing sunset, a sparkling garden or a glistening rainbow. What other ideas can you think of?

C

 Helen Frankenthaler, *Mountains and Sea,* 1952. Oil on canvas, 36 5/8" x 117 1/4" (93 x 298 cm).
Collection of the artist, on extended loan to the National Gallery of Art, Washington, DC.

Artists explore many ways of painting. The two paintings in this lesson have very different colors, lines and shapes. You can also see one thing that makes them alike.

Both of these paintings have colors with soft, fuzzy **edges**. The artists diluted their paints. **Dilute** means adding a liquid such as water. A diluted paint flows and lets you blend colors.

Look at both paintings. Where do the colors **blend**? Can you imagine how each artist created the soft, fuzzy edges?

You can create paintings with a soft, watery look. Try this. Begin your painting on a damp paper. Then put some water on your brush and dip it in paint.

Try different brushstrokes on the damp paper. Let some of the colors blend. If the paper gets too wet, blot up the water with a tissue. As the paint dries, you can add details to your work.

C

Pattern and Rhythm
Explore Brushstrokes

Indji, ***The Rainbow Snake,*** Port Keats Region. 22 1/2 x 10 1/2" (57 x 27 cm). Collection of Louis A. Allen.

Artists use paintbrushes in many ways. An artist in Australia made the painting in picture A. His painting is about the "Dreamtime." A Dreamtime story tells about the beginning of life in Australia.

This painting tells about a giant Rainbow snake that went to the desert. It dug holes to bring up water. Then the snake wiggled across the sand, leaving deep grooves. The grooves filled up with water and became rivers. The water changed the desert into a place where people and other living things could survive.

Picture B shows a small part of this painting. Why is the painting filled with tiny dots? What do the patterns and visual rhythms mean?

 Indji, ***The Rainbow Snake*** (detail).

Henri Matisse, *Purple Robe and Anemones,* 1937. Oil on canvas, 28 3/4 x 23 3/4"
(73 x 60 cm). The Baltimore Museum of Art (The Cone Collection, formed by
Dr. Claribel Cone and Miss Etta Cone of Baltimore, Maryland).

D Student artwork.

The painting in picture C has many kinds of **brushstrokes**. It is filled with patterns that make visual rhythms. Where do you see wavy lines repeated? patterns with straight lines? What other brushstrokes create patterns?

Try different ways to use a paintbrush. Then create a painting with visual rhythms. Make patterns of brushstrokes to create the rhythm. Students created the paintings in picture D. What subjects or themes might you choose?

You have learned that artists use lines, colors and other **elements of design** to express moods or feelings. Use art words to tell what you think about each painting.

These artists have shown light from the sun, moon or stars. The source of light is the **center of interest** in each artwork.

Look at the painting in picture A. What textures do you see? How are they made? What fills up most of the space in the painting? Why? What else do you see? Have you ever seen a sky like this? How do the lines, colors and shapes make you feel?

Does the painting in picture B show a sunset or sunrise? How do the lines, colors and shapes in this painting help to give you a special feeling? What else did the artist want you to see and feel?

 Vincent van Gogh, *The Starry Night,* 1889. Oil on canvas, 29 x 36 1/4" (74 x 92 cm). Collection, The Museum of Modern Art, New York (Acquired through the Lillie P. Bliss Bequest).

B **John Marin,** *Sunset, Casco Bay.* Wichita Art Museum, Wichita, Kansas (The Roland P. Murdock Collection). Photograph: Henry Nelson.

Does the scene in picture C look like a real or imaginary place? What lines, colors and shapes do you see? What special feelings do you get from the design? Why?

Show what you have learned. Create a picture of a real or imaginary place. Show how light and color can make a place look and feel very special. What design elements will you use? What will your center of interest be?

 Charles Burchfield, *Sun and Rocks,* 1918–50. Gouache and watercolor on paper, 40 x 56" (101 x 142 cm). Albright-Knox Art Gallery, Buffalo, New York (Room of Contemporary Art Fund, 1953).

 Church, Friendly Cove, ca. 1930. Courtesy of British Columbia Provincial Museum.

 Emily Carr, *Indian Church (Friendly Cove),* 1929. Oil on canvas, 42 3/4 x 27 1/8" (109 x 69 cm). Art Gallery of Ontario, Toronto (Bequest of Charles S. Band, 1970).

 Photograph of subject used by Stuart Davis in his ***Summer Landscape,*** 1930. Collection, The Museum of Modern Art, New York.

Artists get ideas for pictures in many ways. In this unit, you will explore ideas for art. You will create art about people, places and animals. You will explore other ideas too.

Emily Carr, a Canadian artist, created the painting in picture A.

Her idea came from a visit to the place shown in picture B. She chose interesting parts of the scene for her painting. She changed and left out some parts of the actual scene. How is her painting of the church different from the photograph?

Compare the photograph in picture C and the painting in picture D. How did the artist make his painting look interesting?

Sketch some scenes near your home or school. Make and use a **viewfinder** to choose the scenes (see picture E). Use your best sketch to create an artwork. In the artwork, show the most important or interesting parts of the scene.

E

 A **Claude Monet, *Waterloo Bridge,*** 1903. Oil on canvas, 25 3/4 x 36 5/8" (64 x 93 cm). Worcester Art Museum, Massachusetts.

Artists create paintings with light and dark colors. They mix white or black paint with other colors to create many new colors.

Shades are dark colors. A **shade** is a color with black added to it. Begin with a color. Add dots of black to the color. Mix the paint. What happens when you add more black?

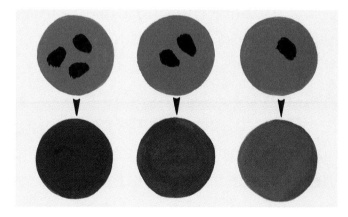

B

C

Tints are light colors. A **tint** is a color with white added to it. When you mix a tint, always begin with the white paint. Do you know why?

D Pierre Bonnard, *Two Dogs in a Deserted Street,* 1894. Wood, 13 7/8 x 10 5/8" (35 x 27 cm). National Gallery of Art, Washington, DC (Ailsa Mellon Bruce Collection).

Artists mix tints and shades so they can express moods and feelings. Why did the artist use many shades for the painting in picture A? What mood comes from the many tints in picture D?

Practice mixing tints and shades. When you mix a tint or shade, you are changing the **value** of the color. For example, pink is a light value of red. A dark value of red is often called maroon.

When the Wind Blows
Watercolor Painting

 A   **C.W. Jefferys,** *Wheat Stacks on the Prairies,* 1907. Oil on canvas, 23 x 35" (58 x 89 cm). Government of Ontario Art Collection, Toronto (Purchase from the artist). Photograph: Tom Moore Photography, Toronto.

How does the wind feel when it is blowing hard? How do the paintings in this lesson capture a feeling of wind blowing?

Look at the painting in picture A. The brushstrokes in the clouds swirl and curve. Find the light and dark colors in the haystacks. How do the **shadows** in the haystacks help to show motion?

Now look at the painting in picture B. The winds of a hurricane are blowing the palm trees. What brushstrokes and colors help to express a windy, stormy feeling?

Students created the paintings in picture C. How did they use brushstrokes and mix colors to capture the feeling of wind?

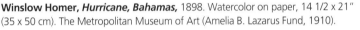

B **Winslow Homer, *Hurricane, Bahamas,*** 1898. Watercolor on paper, 14 1/2 x 21" (35 x 50 cm). The Metropolitan Museum of Art (Amelia B. Lazarus Fund, 1910).

C Student artwork.

The artworks in pictures B and C are painted with **watercolor paint**. Watercolor paints come in small trays. You dip your brush in water. Then you gently rub the brush on the tray of paint.

To make a tint with watercolor paints, use white paper. When you apply the paint, the white paper makes the color look like a tint. Your tempera, or poster paints, can also be used with a lot of water (see Lesson 14).

Think about a time when you saw and felt the wind blowing very hard. Make a painting to share your memory of that time.

 J.E.H. MacDonald, *Leaves in the Brook,* ca.1918. Oil on pressed board, 8 1/4 x 10 5/8" (21 x 27 cm).
McMichael Canadian Art Collection (Gift of Mr. A.Y. Jackson, 1966).

Imagine you could walk into the scenes in these paintings. What would you expect to hear or touch? What would you like to do or explore?

Each painting shows a different season. These artists show some of the colors, spaces and moods in nature.

In picture A, Canadian artist J. E. H. MacDonald shows autumn

leaves in a brook. The **space** in the picture is filled with autumn-like colors. What else can you see and describe?

What is the **color scheme**, or plan, for this painting? Are most of the colors warm or cool? Why? An artist would say this painting has a warm, dark color scheme. Even the browns look "warm." Many of the browns are mixed from yellow, red and a small amount of blue.

B Howard Storm, *Winter House,* 1980. Oil on canvas, 26 x 26" (66 x 66 cm). Courtesy of the artist.

C Claude Monet, *Meadow at Giverny.* Oil on canvas, 36 1/4 x 32 1/8" (92 x 82 cm). Museum of Fine Arts, Boston (Juliana Cheney Edwards Collection).

In picture B, Howard Storm shows a winter landscape. How has he used the picture space?

This winter landscape has a monochromatic color scheme. **Monochromatic** means one color. Why do you think the artist used many tints and shades of blue?

The landscape in picture C was painted by Claude Monet. This scene was near his home in France. How has he planned spaces to show the sky, trees and sunny meadow?

The main colors in this painting are related, or analogous. Related colors are next to each other on the color wheel (see page 33). Can you identify the related colors in this painting? What mood do the colors help to express?

Think about the season you like best. How will you plan the colors and spaces? What ideas and feelings can your artwork show?

Color in Landscapes
Shading and Detail

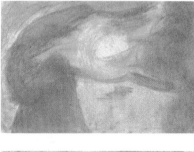

A

When you see your world as an artist, you notice subtle differences in colors. **Subtle** means that you can see small changes or differences. Look at the photograph of clouds in picture A. Where do you see subtle colors?

You can create subtle colors in your artwork. Shading is one way. **Shading** is a gradual change from light to dark. You can also create shading by blending related colors, such as yellow, orange and red. Students created the shaded drawings in picture B.

B   Student artwork.

 Camille Pissarro, *Orchard in Bloom, Louveciennes,* 1872. Oil on canvas, 17 3/4 x 21 5/8″ (45 x 55 cm). The National Gallery of Art, Washington, DC (Ailsa Mellon Bruce Collection).

Artists also learn to see details. **Details** are small shapes that show how one thing is different from another. Look for details in picture C. How do the details help you see the differences in the trees? What other details do you see?

Look at some of the artwork you have made. Study the colors and details. Can you improve your artwork by using subtle colors and more details?

Many artists have created artworks about animals. They have shown pets, farm animals and wildlife.

Picture A is a **portrait**, or likeness, of a real dog named Brizo. Rosa Bonheur, an artist from France, painted the picture about 130 years ago.

BRIZO.

Rosa Bonheur, *Brizo, A Shepherd's Dog,* 1864.
Oil on canvas, 13 1/4 x 15" (46 x 33 cm).
Reproduced by permission of the Trustees,
The Wallace Collection, London.

Look at the texture of the dog's hair. If you could pet the real dog, would the hair feel soft or rough? How can you tell? What kind of brushstrokes create the textures?

Now squint your eyes just a little and look at this painting.

Squinting helps you see the **values**, or light and dark areas, in the painting. Where has the artist used shades, or dark values? Where has the artist used tints, or light values? Why did the artist use light and dark colors?

 Student artwork.

B John James Audubon, *American Flamingo,* Plate CCCCXXXI, No. 87, from *The Birds of America*, 1838. Hand-colored engraving with aquatint, 38 x 26" (97 x 66 cm). National Gallery of Art, Washington, DC (Gift of Mrs. Walter B. James).

John James Audubon created the artwork in picture B. He was born in Haiti but he lived in the United States. He created paintings of over 1,000 birds. His paintings are in a book called *The Birds of America*.

Where do you see tints and shades in picture B? Why do the changes in light and dark colors help you see textures? What else do you see?

Students created the two paintings in picture C. What did they show? How?

Sketch one of your favorite animals. Give the animal a special pose or expression. Then create a painting of it. Mix tints and shades and show the textures of the animal.

51

 Unknown, *Raven Addressing Assembled Animals,* ca. 1590, India-Mughul School.
Reproduced by Courtesy of the Trustees of The British Museum, London.

People in many lands write and **illustrate** stories about animals. The painting in picture A is from India. It illustrates a story about animals. Many animals have gathered to hear a raven speak.

A raven is a very big bird. It looks like a crow. It is the center of interest in this painting. Where do you see the raven? Why are most of the animals looking toward it?

There are many animals in this painting. Some are imaginary creatures. Can you find them? What other animals do you see? Can you tell if they are listening or speaking?

Several artists created paintings like this. They worked together as a team. One designed the background and largest shapes. Some artists worked on the realistic animals. Others worked on the imaginary animals. Are there other ways artists could work together?

With other students in your class, create a large picture, or **mural**, about real or imaginary

 Student artwork.

animals. You could make up a story to illustrate.

Plan the background first and paint it. List the animals, trees or other shapes that you need. Draw and cut out these shapes. Try several ways to place the shapes. Then paste the shapes down.

53

Some artists make **prints** by carving a design in a block of wood. They put ink on the wood and press paper on the ink. The design on the block of wood can be printed again and again. The print of the insect in picture A was made in this way.

You can make prints from a block of clay. Make a thick, smooth block.

Draw an insect on the smooth clay. Use a paper clip to carve into the clay. The lines and shapes must be wide and deep. Follow the steps in pictures B and D.

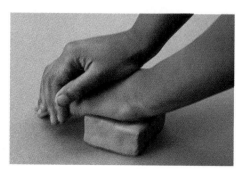

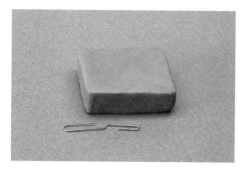

Bug   3/10   C. Kelley

 A

B

 Student artwork.

A student made this print of a grasshopper. He signed his print as artists do. He gave his print a title.

The print has two numbers. The 1 tells you this was the first print he made. The 3 tells you he made three prints like this one.

D

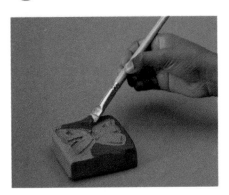

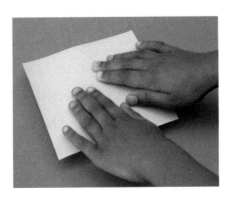

1. Brush paint or printing ink on the flat parts of the block.

2. Put paper over the block. Rub the back of the paper.

3. Carefully lift the paper. Let your print dry.

 Vincent van Gogh, *Old Man Grieving*, 1882. 20 x 12 1/4" (50 x 31 cm). Van Gogh Museum, Amsterdam.

 J. B. Brown, *Boy Playing Piccolo,* 1885. Etching, 20 x 14" (127 x 36 cm). Butler Institute of American Art, Youngstown, Ohio (Gift of Mrs. M. J. Sampson).

There are many ways to see and think about art. The artworks in this lesson show people in different poses. A **pose** is a special way to stand or sit.

Study the figures, or people, in these artworks. Take the same pose that you see in each picture. Imagine how it feels to be posing for the artist. Tell what each person might think or feel.

Now imagine you are the artist who created each picture. Study the **angles**, or bends, in each figure. Where do you see similar bends in your own body?

George Bellows, *Lady Jean,* 1924. Black lithographic crayon on white paper, 22 x 13" (56 x 35 cm). The Fogg Art Museum, Harvard University, Cambridge, Massachusetts (Bequest of Meta and Paul J. Sachs).

George Bellows, *Lady Jean,* 1924. Oil on canvas, 72 x 36" (183 x 91 cm). Yale University Art Gallery, New Haven, Connecticut (Bequest of Stephen C. Clark).

The bends in a figure show proportions. A **proportion** is the size of one part in relation to another. For example, the upper part of an arm is about the same length as the lower part. What other proportions in a figure can you discover?

Compare the sketch in picture C and the painting in picture D. What proportions do you see? Why did the artist make the sketch before the painting?

Make sketches of students who pose for your class. Show the bends in the body and the proportions.

A **Ben Shahn,** *Handball,* 1939. Tempera on paper over composition board, 22 3/4 x 31 1/4" (58 x 79 cm). Collection, The Museum of Modern Art, New York (Abby Aldrich Rockefeller Fund).

Where do you play and have fun outside? What games and activities do you enjoy with friends? Have you ever stopped playing and looked at people who are near or far away from you? What did you notice?

Look at the painting in picture A. The artist has shown two players who look near to you. These players are large and close to the bottom of the painting. The other players are small and higher up in the picture. This makes them look far away.

When artists show things that are near or far away, they are using **perspective**.

 William Glackens, *Bathing at Bellport, Long Island,* 1911. Oil on canvas, 26 1/16 x 32" (66 x 81 cm). The Brooklyn Museum (Bequest of Laura L. Barnes).

Now look at the painting in picture B. The people who look far away are small. The people who look near are larger and closer to the bottom of the picture.

You can use these ideas about perspective. Remember: When you want to show something is near, draw it large and close to the bottom of your picture. When you want to show something is farther away, draw it smaller and higher up in the picture.

Create a picture of a place outdoors where you like to have fun with other people. How can you show things in perspective?

59

A Crowded Scene
Space and Expression

A   **Everett Shinn,** ***The Monologist,*** 1910. Pastel on paper, 8 1/4 x 11 3/4" (21 x 30 cm). Wichita Art Museum, Wichita, Kansas
(The Roland P. Murdock Collection). Photograph: Henry Nelson.

Have you ever been on a stage and seen the audience? Have you ever seen crowds of people in other places? How can you show this kind of scene in an artwork?

Imagine you are the artist who is drawing the scene in picture A. Where would the artist be on the stage? Why did the artist draw the actor so large? Why did the artist draw the people in the first rows larger than the people in the back rows?

Now look at picture B. The largest shape is the person on the stage. Why do the people in the audience look smaller?

In both artworks, the artist created a feeling of **space** and

Jacob Lawrence, *Concert,* 1950. Tempera on paper, 22 x 30" (56 x 76 cm). Wichita Art Museum, Wichita, Kansas (The Roland P. Murdock Collection). Photograph: Henry Nelson.

distance. The sizes of the shapes help you to see what is near and far away.

You can also show distance by overlapping shapes. **Overlap** means that one shape looks like it is behind another one. Can you find some of the overlapping shapes in both artworks?

Think about places where you see a crowd of people. Begin your picture by drawing the people near to you in the scene. Draw them very large on your paper. How can you show the people who are farther away?

26 *Faces of People*
Proportion and Expression

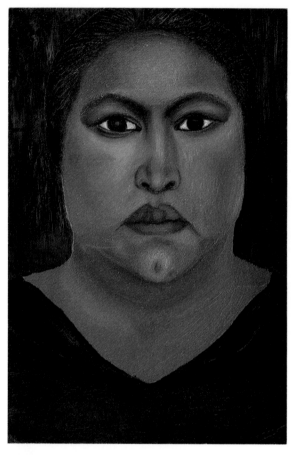

 Angel Torres Jaramillo (TEBO), *Portrait of My Mother,* 1937. Oil on cardboard, 9 1/8 x 6 1/8" (23 x 16 cm). Collection, The Museum of Modern Art, New York (The Latin American Collection, Gift of Sam A. Lewisohn).

 Ben Shahn, *Dr. J. Robert Oppenheimer,* 1954. Brush and ink, 19 1/2 x 12 1/4" (50 x 31 cm). Collection, The Museum of Modern Art, New York (Purchase).

The artworks in this lesson are portraits. A **portrait** shows a likeness of a person. These portraits also tell about the feelings or moods of people.

What **expressions** do you see on each face? An expression might be happy, sad, angry or tired. What parts of a face help to give it an expression?

A portrait also helps you know if a person is young or old, fat or thin. How do these artworks help you see these differences in people? What other differences do you see in each artwork?

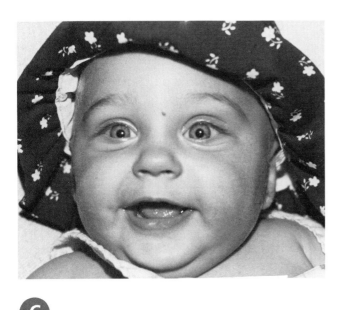

C

D

E Student artwork.

You can draw portraits. Sit across from a classmate. Study the shape of his or her head. Draw this shape very large. Then sketch guidelines similar to the dotted lines in picture D. These lines help you remember some proportions. For example, the eyes are about halfway between the bottom of the chin and the top of the head.

Now ask your classmate to pose with a special expression. Finish your drawing by showing exactly how your classmate looks!

A student your age created the portrait in picture E. Do you think the artwork shows a special expression? Why or why not?

63

27

Portraits and Self-Portraits
Painting

A   **Robert Henri, *Eva Green,*** 1907. Oil on canvas, 24 1/8 x 20 3/16" (61 x 51 cm). Wichita Art Museum, Wichita, Kansas (The Roland P. Murdock Collection). Photograph: Henry Nelson.

B   ***Portrait of a Boy,*** Egyptian. Encaustic on wood panel, 7 x 15" (19 x 39 cm). The Metropolitan Museum of Art (Gift of Edward S. Harkness, 1918).

You have learned that a portrait shows how a real person looks. A **self-portrait** is an artwork that shows the person who created it. Have you ever painted a portrait or self-portrait?

Look at the paintings in this lesson. Each artist has made the face the center of interest. How have the artists shown the eyes, nose and other details in the faces? What expressions do you see? How have the artists shown the expression on each face?

William H. Johnson, *Jim,* ca. 1930. Oil on canvas, 21 x 18" (53 x 46 cm). National Museum of American Art, Washington, DC (Gift of the Harmon Foundation). Courtesty Art Resource, New York.

Student artwork.

When you paint a portrait, mix one main color for the skin. Paint all the skin areas first. The skin usually shows on the head, neck and shoulders. Then mix other colors for the hair and important details. Can you explain why details are the last parts to paint?

The portraits in pictures A, B and C were created by adult artists. A student created the self-portrait in picture D. She used a mirror to create a drawing. Then she made the painting.

Paint a portrait or a self-portrait. Make the face large and show the neck and shoulders. Remember to paint the skin and other large shapes first. Then paint the details. Why are these steps helpful?

28

Still Lifes of Food
Symbols and Design

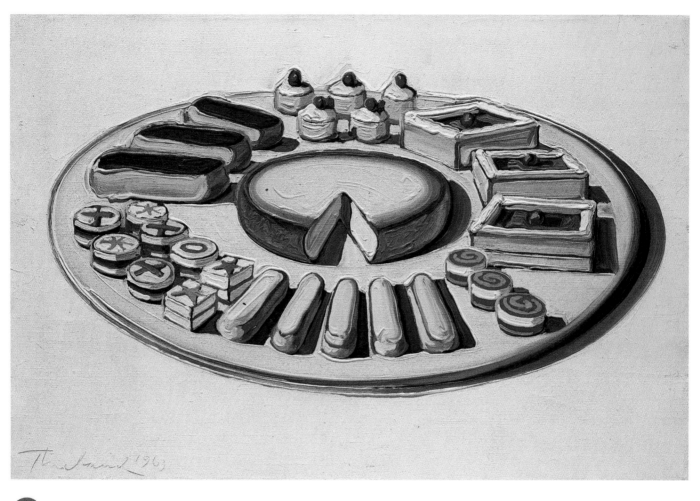

A   **Wayne Thiebaud, *French Pastries,*** 1963. Oil on canvas, 16 x 24" (41 x 61cm). Hirshhorn Museum and Sculpture Garden, Smithsonian Institution, Washington, DC (Gift of Joseph H. Hirshhorn, 1966). Photograph: Lee Stalsworth.

The two paintings in this lesson are still lifes. A **still life** shows objects such as food, shoes, books or dishes on a table. The objects in a still life are often things people admire or use.

The objects in a still life can also be **symbols**. For example, a book may be a symbol for wisdom. Food may be a symbol for health or happiness. Look at the foods in both paintings. What ideas might they stand for?

Why do you think each artist wanted a simple, plain background in the paintings?

How did each artist show the textures of the food? Where do you see shadows in each painting?

Now look at the **space** in each painting. Most of the space is used to show the food. Why did each artist fill up most of the space with the shapes of food?

Create an artwork about your favorite foods. Think about the reasons you like the food. Are some of the foods symbols for ideas? Are they foods you enjoy or need?

Plan your artwork. Use most of the picture space to show the food. What other ideas should you think about?

29 *City Spaces*
Design for Expression

There are many ways to express ideas and feelings in art. The paintings in this lesson show two cities. Each artist sends you special messages by using the **elements of design**. Which painting expresses the feeling of a very busy city? Which painting shows a very quiet town? How can you tell?

 Tarsila do Amaral, *Central Railway of Brazil,* 1924. Oil on canvas, 55 7/8 x 50" (142 x 127 cm). Museu de Arte Contemporânea da Universidade de São Paulo, Brazil.

Let's look at picture A. This artist has used many geometric lines and shapes. **Geometric** lines and shapes have smooth, even edges. What geometric lines and shapes do you see in this painting?

Now look at main directions of lines and shapes. Many of the lines and shapes have **vertical** and **horizontal** edges. Some have gentle curves. These design elements help to create the feeling of a quiet place.

What other design elements do you see? How do they help to give you a special feeling?

Look closely at picture B. Have you ever walked down a busy street like this? Have you ever seen flashing signs or people moving so fast that they look blurred?

 George Grosz, *Dallas Broadway,* 1952. Watercolor on paper, 19 1/2 x 15 1/2" (49 x 39 cm). University Art Collection, Southern Methodist University, Dallas, Texas (Gift of Leon A. Harris, Jr.).

Notice how the main lines and shapes are **diagonal**, or slanting. The edges of many shapes are also fuzzy or uneven. These design elements help you see and feel the motions in a busy place.

What other design elements create the feeling of a busy place? For example, what are the main colors and textures? How are they different from the colors and textures in picture A?

Create a picture about your neighborhood or town. Will you make your picture look very quiet and calm or full of action? What design elements can help you express your ideas?

A City at Night
Contrasts in Color

 Tom Bacher, *Mount Adams (In the Light),* 20th century. Phosphorescent acrylic on canvas, 24 x 30" (61 x 76 cm). Cincinnati Art Galleries.

Do you like to see the lights in city buildings at night? At night, you see the **contrast**, or difference, between very dark and very bright colors.

Tom Bacher loves to see the contrasting colors in a city at night. In pictures A and B, you see one of his paintings of a city.

This artwork is created with a special kind of paint. The paint absorbs, or soaks up, light. His paint is similar to "glow in the dark" paints.

Picture A shows how his painting looks in daylight. Picture B shows how the same painting glows in a dark room. Which design has more contrast in the colors? What other differences do you see?

 Tom Bacher, *Mount Adams (In the Dark),* 20th century. Phosphorescent acrylic on canvas, 24 x 30" (61 x 76 cm). Cincinnati Art Galleries.

Create an artwork that shows your home, school or neighborhood at night. You can create strong contrasts by drawing on dark paper with bright colors of oil pastel.

You might create a resist painting. Use wax or oil crayons on white paper. Press hard to make a thick layer of each color. When the drawing is finished, brush a dark color of watercolor paint over the whole paper. Use a wide brush. The paint will **resist**, or roll away from, the parts you've colored.

B   ***Brooklyn Bridge.*** Photograph: Wayne Andrews.

A   **Samuel Halpert, *Brooklyn Bridge,*** 1913. Oil on canvas, 34 x 42" (86 x 107 cm). Collection of Whitney Museum of American Art, New York (Gift of Mr. and Mrs. Benjamin Halpert). Photograph: Geoffrey Clements.

C   **Brett Weston, *Brooklyn Bridge.***

All of the artworks in this lesson show the Brooklyn Bridge in New York City. The Brooklyn Bridge was designed by John Roebling more than 100 years ago. Many artists have created pictures about the bridge.

Each artist has seen and thought about the bridge in a special way. Each artist created an **original**, or different, artwork about the same subject.

You are learning to see and discuss art like an expert. Show what you have learned. Take time to look at the pictures in this lesson. Study the different views of the bridge. Which artworks do you like? Why? Make up your own mind.

 John Marin, *Brooklyn Bridge,* 1912. Watercolor, 15 1/2 x 18 1/2" (39 x 47 cm). The Metropolitan Museum of Art, New York (The Alfred Stieglitz Collection).

 Joseph Stella, *Brooklyn Bridge, Variation on an Old Theme,* 1939. Oil on canvas. Collection of Whitney Museum of American Art, New York.

Choose the artwork you like best. Tell what you see in the artwork. Use art words you know. Tell why you chose the work. Then find out which artworks your classmates chose.

You can also create art in your own way. Help to choose a subject that everyone in the class will draw.

After the subject is chosen, create an original picture about it. Original means that your picture will be very different from others.

Art in Your World
Living with Art

B Photograph of Francisco Mora.
Photograph: Juan Mora.

A Photograph: Ann Hawthorne for the Penland School.

Do you know people who draw, paint or create other kinds of art? Where do they create art?

The man and woman in picture A create metal trays, cups and jewelry. They use hammers, saws and other tools to create the metal forms. Artists who use a material skillfully are **craftsworkers**.

Artists use different tools and materials for their work. The artist in picture B is creating a painting. An **easel** holds the painting so it is easy to see and work on. The artist holds a **palette**, a tray for mixing paint. He will display his best artwork in an art gallery or museum.

The students in picture C are in an art museum. A museum has authentic artworks. An **authentic**

artwork is one the artist makes. It is not a copy made by someone else. Where else can you see authentic artworks in your community?

Many artists work on designs for toys, cars and other things people need or buy. Artists also design motion pictures and television shows.

The artist in picture D is making a storyboard. A **storyboard** has drawings of each scene in a motion picture. The storyboard includes words that actors will speak. The words are under each drawing. A storyboard helps everyone plan a motion picture.

The world of art includes many people who have a job, or career, in art. In this unit, you will learn more about art in your world and the people who create it.

31 Industrial Design
Designs People Use

 Melamine Dinnerware, Sticks and Bricks pattern. Courtesy of Copco ® division of Wilton Enterprises.

 Hans J. Wegner, *The Peacock Chair*, 1947 and *The Chair*, 1949. Courtesy of the artist.

Artists design many of the factory-made objects that you see and use. Artists plan the textures you touch. They design the forms you hold. They plan the colors and shapes.

Artists who plan factory-made objects are called **industrial designers**. After an object is designed, the object can be made in a factory. Many people can have objects that have the same design.

Industrial designers planned the objects shown in this lesson. They chose the materials and planned the forms you see, touch or hold.

Look at each picture. What parts of the objects were carefully designed? What makes you think so?

 Courtesy of Culligan International Company, Northbrook, Illinois.

 Duraglide Spiral Slide. Designer: Gerald Beekenkamp. Courtesy of Paris Slides, Inc.

Industrial designers plan radios, bicycles, cars and many other objects. The designer helps to make sure that factory-made objects are safe, attractive and easy to use.

Look for examples of industrial design in newspapers or old magazines. Cut out the pictures and display them. Which designs are the best? How can you decide?

A ***Brookview Plaza roadside sign.*** Designer: Richard Lang. Photograph from *Successful Sign Design.* Reprinted by permission of Retail Reporting Corporation.

B ***Lucky Stores, San Francisco.*** Design: Walker Group/CNI, New York. Photograph: Toshi Yoshimi, from *Successful Food Merchandising and Display.* Reprinted by permission of Retail Reporting Corporation.

Some artists are graphic designers. A **graphic designer** plans the lettering and artwork for signs, books and many other things people read. Graphic is an ancient Greek word. It means you share ideas by writing and drawing. The outdoor sign in picture A is a graphic design. An artist planned the sign and the lettering.

A grocery store has many graphic designs. The designer plans the lettering and pictures on displays and packages. What other graphic designs can you find in picture B?

 Newscenter 4 logo. Designers: Beverly Littlewood and Gary E. Teixeira. Photograph: William A. Sontag. Courtesy of Type Director's Club.

American Museum of Natural History
Central Park West at 79 Street
Open FREE Friday and Saturday evenings 5-9

Made possible by a grant from Mobil

D Ivan Chermayeff, *Poster for American Museum of Natural History,* 1982. Courtesy of Chermayeff and Geismar, Inc.

You see many graphic designs on television. The design in picture C is for a news program on television. What parts of the design did an artist plan? What other graphic designs do you see on television or at home?

Look at the poster in picture D. What parts of the poster did a graphic designer plan? What messages do you get from the poster?

Look for examples of graphic design in your school, home and neighborhood. Create a graphic design that sends an important message to people. Describe how your design helps people understand the message.

33 Picture Writing
Messages from Pictures

Japan United States Southwest Indian Mexico Aztec Africa Egypt

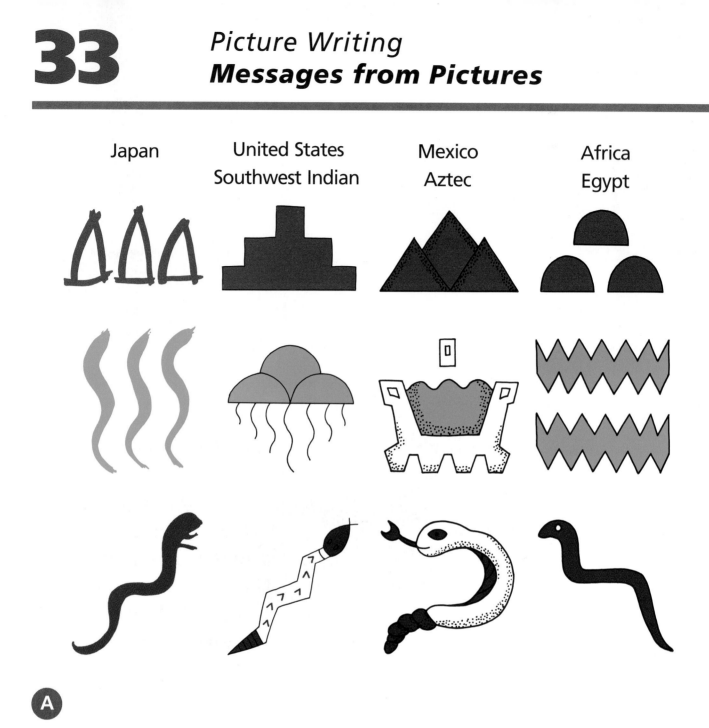

A

Long ago, people began to draw pictures to share ideas. Picture writing became a way for people to tell about things without using words.

People in many lands invented pictures for ideas. Look at the simple pictures in A. Each picture is a visual **symbol** for an idea. What ideas in picture A can you name? How are the visual symbols alike? How are they different?

B

You see picture writing every day. Picture B has symbols that help people understand ideas. Can you tell what these visual symbols mean?

You can share ideas without using words. You can use picture writing. You can invent simple pictures to tell what you mean.

Think of a sentence or command that sends a message. Draw one or more pictures to share your message. Make each picture very simple. Simple means you show only the most important lines and shapes.

Lettering
Picturing the Alphabet

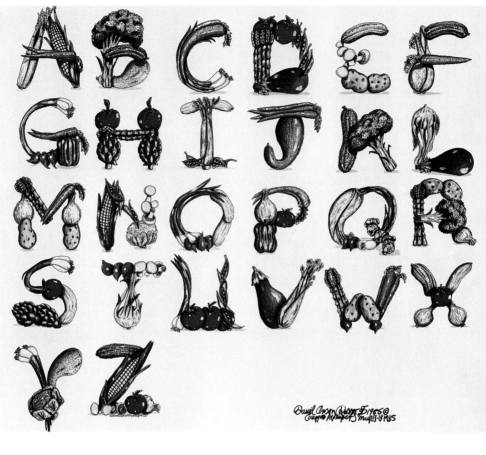

Alphabet vegetables, 1985. © 1991 David Anson Russo.

Graphic designers use letters of the alphabet in many of their artworks. Some graphic designers create **picture alphabets**.

In a picture alphabet, the shape of each letter is also a picture. The designer makes each picture fit the shape of a letter.

Picture alphabets often have related shapes and ideas. For example, in picture A, the picture alphabet is made up of things you can eat.

Look carefully. Do you see ears of corn and carrots? Both of these vegetables have long narrow shapes. Where has the artist used these shapes to create part of a letter? What round shapes did he use to make letters? How are they used?

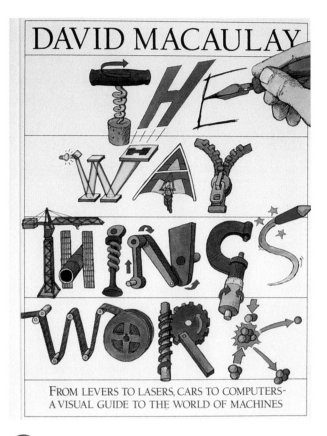

C · **Joseph Volpicelli, *Alphabet.*** Courtesy of Werner Pfeiffer.

Look at the letters on the book cover in picture B. This book is about machines, tools and inventions. Each letter has some shapes from a machine, tool or invention.

Can you find the letter that looks like an open zipper? Where do you see the point of a pen? What other shapes are used to make picture letters?

Your class can make a picture alphabet. Choose a theme everyone can work on. Each student can make one letter for the picture alphabet. When all the artwork is finished, your class can display the whole alphabet. What theme did the artist use for the alphabet in picture C?

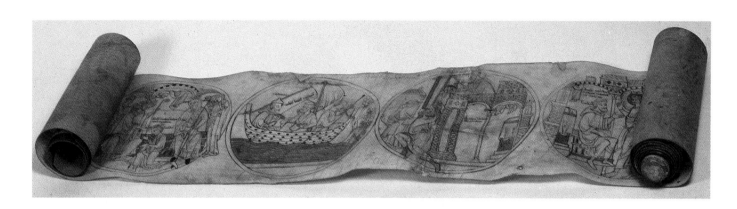

Unknown, *Harley Roll: Scenes from the Life of Saint Guthlac,* 8th century.
Parchment, approximately 120" (305 cm) long. Courtesy of the British Library.

B

Unknown, accordion-folded pages, part of a catalog to the ***Triptaka,*** the canon of Buddhist scriptures, 12th century. Accordion-folded paper printed with inked woodblocks. Courtesy of the British Library.

Have you ever seen books like these? Long ago, people in many lands made their own books by hand. They did not have printed books like you have.

The very old book in picture A is a **scroll**. You unroll the ends to read it. This kind of book was made for thousands of years in many lands.

This scroll is made so you roll the left and right sides. Some scrolls are made so you roll them from the top and bottom.

Picture B shows a book with pages that fold back and forth. This folded book was made in China many years ago. The lettering was printed. Artists carved letters into a block of wood. Then the woodblock was covered with ink and pressed down on the page.

C   **Ed Rossbach, *The Weaver's Secret Book,*** 1977. Mixed print media, accordion-folded, 5 x 5 1/2 x 3/4" (13 x 14 x 2 cm). Courtesy of the Textile Museum.

Some artists still make books by hand. An artist who likes to weave made the book in picture C.

Make a scroll or a folded book. Write and draw in it. What ideas will you include?

A folded book

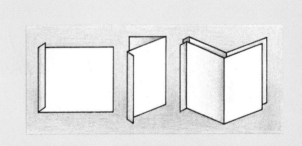

1. Make a narrow fold.
2. Fold in half.
3. Make others.
4. Put glue here.

A scroll

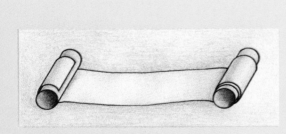

Paper is glued down.
Use tubes or sticks.

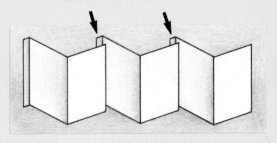

D

E

85

 Photograph of Thomas Feelings.

Black Pilgrimage | Tom Feelings

 Cover illustration from *Black Pilgrimage*. © 1972 Thomas Feelings.

Meet Thomas Feelings. He is an illustrator of books for children. An **illustrator** creates pictures that explain ideas.

Mr. Feelings began to illustrate children's books after a trip to Africa. He works on books that teach people about Africa and African Americans. His illustrations have won prizes.

 Cover illustration from *Tommy Traveler in the World of Black History*. © 1991 Thomas Feelings.

 Cover illustration from *King Krakus and the Dragon*, © 1979 by Janina Domanska. By permission of Greenwillow Books, a division of William Morrow & Co., Inc.

E Interior illustration from *King Krakus and the Dragon*, © 1979 by Janina Domanska. By permission of Greenwillow Books, a division of William Morrow & Co., Inc.

Pictures for books can be done in different **art media**, or art materials. Some illustrators like to use one material, such as markers, for their work. Others like to use different media together, such as paint and chalk.

Illustrations can also be done in different **styles**. Mr. Feelingses' pictures have a realistic style. The illustrations in Ms. Domanska's book are done in the style of fantasy. Why do you think these books have different styles?

Find an illustrated book with pictures you like. Tell why you like the illustrations. Can you write and illustrate a story?

37 Photography
Creating a Sunprint

Anna Atkins, *Lycopodium Flagellatum (Algae),* 1840-50. Blueprint, 11 1/8 x 8 3/16" (28 x 21 cm). Gernsheim Collection, Harry Ransom Humanities Research Center, The University of Texas at Austin.

Picture A is a photogram. A **photogram** is like a photograph. It is a record, or print, of light and shadow made on special paper. Photograms like this one are called sunprints or blueprints.

For this photogram, the artist arranged a plant on special paper. She put the paper in bright light.

The paper made a record of the plant's shadow. Then the artist put the paper in a special liquid. The liquid made the paper turn blue and the shadow turn white.

Photograms are one kind of **photograph**. What kinds of photographs do you know about? Can you explain why a camera is used for many photographs?

 Student artwork.

 Student artwork.

Photograms can be artworks. Look again at picture A. This photogram is not just a record of a plant's shadow. The artist carefully arranged the plant to show the delicate outlines and tiny leaves.

Look at the photograms in pictures B and C. Students made them. Do you think they are artworks? Why or why not?

You can create a photographic artwork. Your teacher will explain how. First, collect objects with interesting edges. The objects must be nearly flat. Some examples are leaves, coins, buttons or yarn.

Arrange the objects on top of stiff paper. Move the objects around. Do the objects suggest ideas? Can you plan a center of interest? What kind of balance will your design have? How else can you plan your artwork?

Film and Television
Pictures That Move

(MUSIC UP)

(SFX: Finger snaps)

SINGERS: *Ooo, Ooo*

I heard it through the grapevine.

Raised in the California sunshine.

ANNCR (VO): California Raisins from the California Vineyards.

SINGERS: *Don't ya know*

I heard it through the grapevine.

ANNCR (VO): Sounds grape, doesn't it?
(MUSIC OUT)

Will Vinton, *Late Show.* Courtesy of California Raisin Advisory Board.

Motion pictures and television are two kinds of art that many people see. In both kinds of art, you see action and movement.

Look at the artwork in picture A. Each scene is part of a movie. Do you know why each picture is slightly different from the next?

  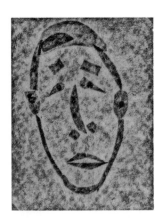 

B Student artwork.

C Student artwork.

Many artists work together to create a movie or television show. There are writers and actors. Some shows have dancers and musicians. Artists design costumes and the sets, or backgrounds, for many shows.

Some movies and television shows have cartoons. The cartoon pictures are drawings but the characters move and speak like people or animals.

Movies and television shows with cartoons are created from many separate pictures. A camera is used to record each picture on a long piece of film or tape. When the film or tape is shown very quickly, you see motion. This kind of art is called an **animation**.

Students created the pictures in B and C. They learned how to create animated pictures with a collage. You can explore this idea.

Cut some eyes and other parts of a face from removable tape. Stick the tape to a background paper. You have made a **collage**. Now make a crayon **rubbing** of the collage.

To make a second picture, carefully remove pieces of the tape, such as an eye and eyebrow. Tape the same shapes on the paper again. Put them in a slightly different place. Make a crayon rubbing of the collage.

Make several faces with different expressions. Then give a name to your animated character.

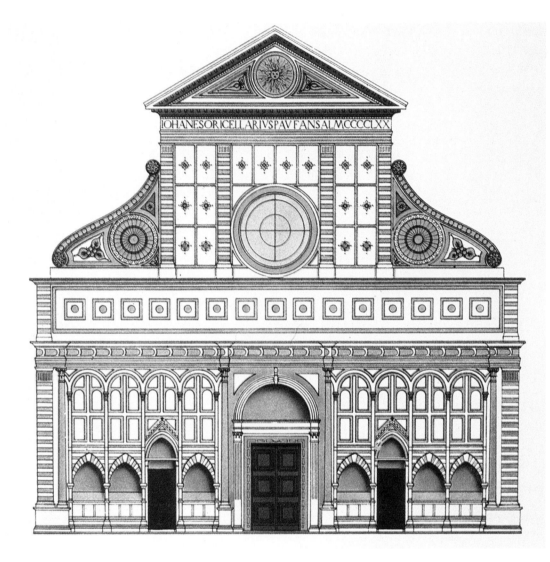

 Alberti, Facade for the Church of Santa Maria Novella, Florence, 1456–1470.

An **architect** is an artist who designs buildings. Many parts of the building must be planned. The exterior, or outside, walls of the building are one part of a plan. The front or main entrance is often the center of interest. The front of a building is called the **facade**.

The facade in picture A was designed over 300 years ago in Italy. The architect's name was Alberti. This facade has a symmetrical design. The left side is just like the right side.

Alberti, Detail of facade for the Church of Santa Maria Novella, Florence.

Look at the shapes in picture B. Can you find them in Alberti's building? Where else do you see shapes inside of other shapes?

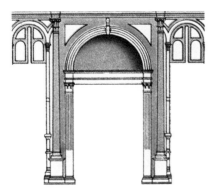

Alberti, Detail of facade for the Church of Santa Maria Novella, Florence.

D Student artwork.

The shapes in picture C are round **arches**. Where do you see round arches in Alberti's building? Round arches were invented about 2,000 years ago by Roman architects. Architecture with many round arches is called **Romanesque**.

Design a symmetrical facade for a building. Fold your paper in half. Cut a large symmetrical shape for the building from paper. Unfold the paper. Then add the details. Details are the shapes of windows, doors and decorations. You can draw or cut shapes for the details.

A *Fountain* (detail), 1980. Paris, France.

B *Empress Theodora and Her Attendants* (detail), 547. Mosaic, San Vitale, Ravenna, Italy. Courtesy of Scala/Art Resource, New York.

Have you ever seen stones placed side-by-side in cement? Have you ever seen a wall with small colorful tiles next to each other? This kind of artwork is called **mosaic**. The mosaic in picture A is on a large fountain in Paris, France.

Hundreds of years ago artists created mosaics for churches in Europe. The mosaic in picture B is made from pieces of glass, marble and gold. These sparkling pictures helped people to remember their beliefs and Bible stories.

C

Mihrab (mosque niche), from the Madrasa Imami, Isfahan, Iran, ca. 1354. Glazed ceramic tiles, 11' 3" (343 cm) high. The Metropolitan Museum of Art, New York (Harris Brisbane Dick Fund).

D   Student artwork.

The mosaic in picture C was created over 600 years ago in Iran. It was made by Islamic artists for their mosque, or place of worship. The designs combine lines from plants and beautiful handwriting.

You can create a collage that looks like a mosaic. Find some old magazines with colorful pages. Neatly tear out some of these pages.

Cut the colored parts of each page into strips about as wide as your thumb. Stack several strips neatly and cut across them to make squares. You can cut other shapes, too.

Sketch several ideas for a mosaic. Your design might show your name, a plant or animal. What other ideas can you try out? What is the best way to glue down your pieces of paper? What design elements should you remember?

A Atrium interior. Courtesy of Allward + Gouinlock, Inc., Ontario, Canada.

B Courtesy of Roger Brooks & Associates.

Architects plan buildings so the light inside is beautiful during the day. They design the shapes and sizes of windows so daylight comes into many rooms. Most people like to see daylight and look out of a window. The building in picture A has a glass roof that allows daylight to come into the space.

Architects also try to plan buildings that are beautiful at night. Do you like to see buildings with lights glowing at night? The light you see often comes from the **interior**, or inside, of the building. In picture B, the light flows through the glass in the windows or doors. You can see the bright shapes glowing at night.

C Rivercenter, San Antonio, Texas. Photograph from *Successful Sign Design.* Reprinted by permission of Retail Reporting Corporation.

D Student artwork.

Some buildings have colorful lights on the **exterior**, or outside. Picture C shows a building at night. You can see lights on the exterior of the building. Where do you see light from the interior spaces?

You can think like an architect. Draw a building. Plan the shapes of the windows and doors carefully. You might add some lampposts or signs.

After your drawing is done, color the windows and other places where the light would be glowing at night. Use wax crayons or oil pastels. Press hard so the color is thick.

Then make your drawing a night scene. Brush dark blue or black watercolor over the whole paper. The watercolor will roll away from, or resist, the parts you have colored. Your drawing will glow with light.

97

42 *Interior Design*
A Colorful Window

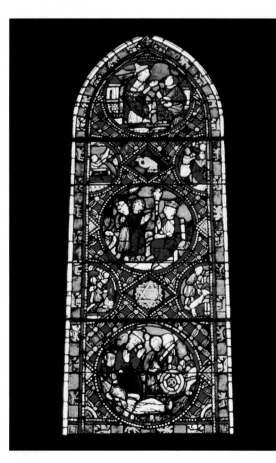

B *Angelika Traylor, **Magic Carpet No. IX.*** Stained glass, 33 x 33"
(84 x 84 cm). © Angelika Traylor.

A ***Episodes from the Life of St. Catherine of
Alexandria,*** 1290. Stained and painted glass, oak,
29 x 81" (74 x 216 cm). The Nelson-Atkins Museum
of Art, Kansas City, Missouri.

Artists work with color and light in many ways. Long ago in Europe, artists made **stained-glass** windows for large churches. When people are inside the church, they see the glowing colors.

Picture A shows one of these windows. It is made from pieces of colored glass. The glass is held together with strips of metal. Colored glass is transparent. **Transparent** means the light shines through it.

You may have seen stained glass in homes, restaurants or libraries. Picture B is an example of present-day stained glass. Today, some artists use transparent plastic instead of glass. Have you seen artwork made from transparent materials? Where?

You can experiment with transparent colors. One way is shown on the next page. Can you think of other experiments?

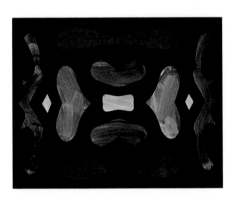

C

1. Cut a piece of dark paper and a clear plastic folder the same size.

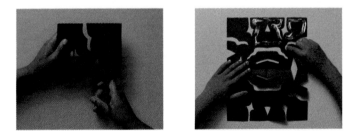

2. Fold the paper twice. Cut shapes from the folded edges. Open the paper. Put paste on one side of the paper. Put the paper inside the folder.

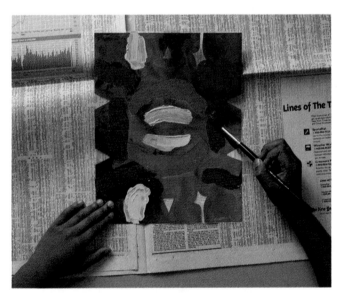

3. Put the folder on newspaper so the pasted side of the paper is facing you. Brush paint on the plastic. Repeat some colors to unify the design. When the paint dries, the design shows from the front.

Display your work in a window. How is it like stained glass? How is it different?

 Chateau Chambord, Loire-et-Char, France, 1519.

The large house in picture A is a castle in France. Castles were built long ago in many lands. People lived in the castles so they could be safe. Sometimes castles were near villages. Many castles had towers. The towers let people see the land around the castle.

Castles and other buildings have **forms**. Forms are thick. You can see them from the top, bottom and many sides. Forms like cones and cylinders make the towers of castles. What forms can you see in pictures A, B and D?

cone　pyramid　sphere

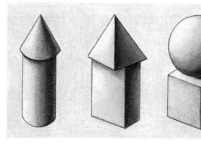

cylinder　slab　cube

 Castle of Muiden, The Netherlands, 13th century. Courtesy of Benelux Press.

You can make a model of a castle or a tower. Find some tubes or small boxes. Make other forms from paper. Use tape and glue to join your forms. Do you see how?

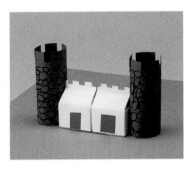

 Neuschwanstein, Germany, 1869–1886. Architects: Eduard Riedell and Georg Von Dollman. Photograph: Mike Horwell/ International Stock Photography.

You can glue and tape forms together.

You can make forms from paper.

Can you make a cone?

Architecture
Styles of Buildings

 Parthenon, model. The Metropolitan Museum of Art, New York.

The people who settled in North America brought ideas from many lands. Some of their ideas about art came from ancient Greece and Rome.

Many buildings in Europe and North America have forms like buildings in ancient Greece and Rome. Picture A is a model of the Parthenon, a building constructed about 2,400 years ago in Athens, Greece.

B Frank Furness, *East pediment of the exterior of the Philadelphia Museum of Art,* 1839–1912. Philadelphia Museum of Art, Pennsylvania. Photograph: Eric Mitchell, 1980.

The building in picture B is in the United States. It is part of the Philadelphia Museum of Art. How is it like the Parthenon? How is it different? There are similar buildings in many large cities in North America. Can you explain why?

Do some research on styles of **architecture** in your community. Draw a picture of a building with design ideas that go back to another country and time.

Picture C is a model of the Pantheon, a building constructed over 1,800 years ago in Rome, Italy.

Pantheon, model. The Metropolitan Museum of Art, New York.

Thomas Jefferson, *Monticello,* west garden facade, 1768-1809. Charlottesville, Virginia.

Julia Morgan, *La Casa Grande*, 1922–1937. Courtesy of Hearst Monument. Photograph: John Blades.

Thomas Jefferson, a United States president, was also an architect. He designed the building in picture D. How is it like the Pantheon? How is it different?

Julia Morgan was one of the first women in North America to become an architect. She designed the Spanish-style mansion in picture E. The mansion is now used as an art museum. It is in California. Why do you think she used ideas from buildings in Spain?

103

Landscape Architecture
A Playground Design

A Sculpture garden of Patsy and Raymond Nasher. Photograph: © Hickey-Robertson Photography, Houston.

Some architects plan parks, gardens and other outdoor spaces. These artists are **landscape architects**.

The lovely garden in picture A was carefully planned. What parts do you think the landscape architect designed?

B *Castle Climber IV.* Courtesy of Rainbow Playground Mfg. Co.

Some landscape architects design playgrounds. They decide where to put the lawns and places to play. They plan the places for trees, fences and shelters. Can you think of other things to plan for a fun, safe and attractive playground?

Your class can design a park or playground. You can show your design in a mural, or large picture.

Plan the ideas for your park. Will it have trees and gardens? Will it have a pond and trails to walk? Will it have places to play or have picnics?

Paint or color a background on mural paper. Draw and cut out the shapes for your design. Plan where you will paste the shapes for your landscape design.

Many artists help plan parts of a community or city. **City planners** are artists who help people make choices about the design of a city. Good choices help make a city a nice place to live.

Look at the pictures on this page and discuss the questions. This will help you think like a city planner.

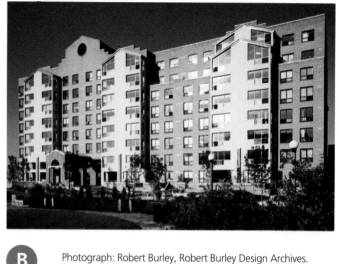

B Photograph: Robert Burley, Robert Burley Design Archives.

What makes a business district nice to visit?

What are some ways to arrange houses and apartments?

A

 Grain elevator. Superstock, Inc.

 Photograph courtesy of the San Antonio Parks & Recreation Department, Texas.

Where should big factories be located?

Where should parks and playgrounds be located?

Courtesy of CN Real Estate, Canada.

A good design for a city includes places for people to live and work. It has places for people to play and shop. It has streets and walks so people can travel. These and other parts of a city should be safe, attractive and work together.

Think about parts of your city that are well-designed. Discuss why. Then create an artwork that shows the good design in your city. Display your artworks. Invite other students to agree or disagree with your ideas about good design.

Around the world, people create art. Some art is part of a tradition. A **tradition** is something people have remembered for a long time.

 Nitobe Memorial Garden, Vancouver, British Columbia.

A *Kente Cloth* (detail). Ashanti tribe, Ghana. Photograph: Jacqueline Robinson.

In some African villages, men weave strips of cloth with beautiful designs. Strips are stitched together to make clothing. This kind of weaving is a tradition.

In Japan, people have a tradition of keeping beautiful gardens. Some of the plants are carefully trimmed to look like sculpture. A gardener from Japan designed the traditional garden in picture B. This garden is in Canada.

D   **Unknown, _Star of Bethlehem Quilt_**, ca. 1830. Cotton. New York State Historical Association, Cooperstown.

C   **Tatipai Barsa, _Ringtail Possum,_** 1991. Acrylic on paper, 22 x 30" (56 x 76 cm). Courtesy of Derek Simpkins Gallery of Tribal Art.

The quilt in picture D was created over 150 years ago. Quilts are made from scraps of cloth. Quiltmaking is a tradition in some families. Sometimes the designs honor important people or events.

Does your family have special traditions? Do you create or use special artwork to keep the tradition? Why?

In this unit, you will learn about art made from different materials. You will learn about art created to celebrate special times and to express ideas. You will learn how artists work with traditional ideas and new ideas about art.

A native artist from Australia created the painting in picture C. His artwork shows plants and animals from traditional stories. Some native artists create similar paintings on tree bark. They make paints from colored clay.

A Rose Kimewon (Williams), *Tufted, quilled, lidded box,* 1979-81. Birchbark, quills, sweetgrass, dye, thread, 3 1/8 x 6 1/4" (8 x 16 cm). Photograph: Bobby Hansson.

B **Calvin Begay and Wilbert Muskett, Jr.,** *Jewel Case, Canyon Collection.* Courtesy of B.G. Mudd Limited and Dick Ruddy Commercial Photography, Albuquerque, New Mexico.

Artists in many lands create fancy boxes and other containers. These artworks often express ideas about the artist's **culture**.

A North American Indian of the Ottawa tribe created the box in picture A. She used natural materials from the woodlands near her home in Canada.

The lid of her box has shapes from a star and a flower. The lid has a radial design that moves out from the center. The star and flower shapes express her respect for nature. What other parts of the design help to express this idea?

The Zuni Indians have a tradition of making art from silver and colorful stones. These materials are mined in New Mexico, where many Zuni people live.

Zuni artists created the box in picture B. The symbol in the center of the lid represents "Father Sun." The pattern around the top three edges symbolizes feathers. The feathers lift prayers to Father Sun. What other symbols can you see? What might they mean?

Stationery Box "Fumi Bako", Korea, 19th century. Cut paper, appliqué, stenciled paint, handpaint, 5 x 17 x 10" (13 x 43 x 25 cm). Collection of Yamane Washi Shiryokan, Totori, Japan.

The box in picture C was made in Korea. It is used to hold things for writing letters. These boxes are made by gluing layers of paper together. This process, or technique, is called **papier-mâché**.

The boxes are finished with colored paper. Sometimes the box has a painted or stenciled design.

The triangles in this box move toward a circle, creating a **radial** design. This circle is a symbol for unity in all living things. Red and yellow are traditional colors for the rising and setting sun.

Find an empty box and decorate it in a special way. Think about the way you can use the box. What symbols could you use in your design? How can you arrange all the parts of your design?

A   *Vest*, front view, 19th century. Courtesy of Hogan Gallery, Inc., Florida. Photograph: Ed Chappell, Inca.

B   *Vest*, back view, 19th century. Courtesy of Hogan Gallery, Inc., Florida. Photograph: Ed Chappell, Inca.

For thousands of years, people have designed and made their own clothing. About one hundred years ago, a Sioux Indian created the vest in pictures A and B. It was worn for special ceremonies.

Long ago, the Sioux Indians made clothing and tents from the hides of animals. The vest has symbols for their way of life in the plains. What symbols can you identify?

The design on the front of the vest in picture A has **symmetrical balance**. Symmetry means that the left side looks like the right side. Each side of the design is like a mirror image of the other.

The back of the vest, in picture B, is nearly symmetrical. Two buffalo are facing each other. A large bird is centered near the top, inside of flowers on vines.

РАБОТЫ СТЕПАНОВОЙ

C Designs for sports clothing, 1923. © Varvara Stepanova.

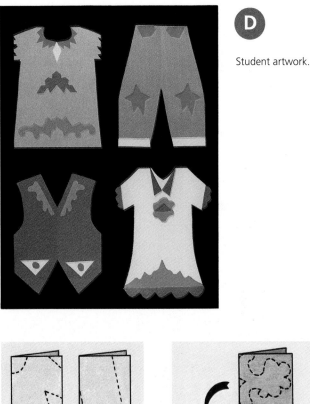

D

Student artwork.

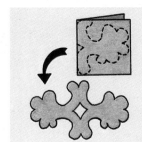

E

Many people today buy their clothing in stores. Artists create the designs for manufactured clothing. These artists are called **clothing designers** or fashion designers.

An artist from Russia created the designs for sports clothes in picture C. She designed the clothes over seventy years ago. Do you think these are still good designs?

Why or why not?

Students created the clothing designs in picture D. They sketched ideas first. They cut a large symmetrical shape for their clothing. Then they cut smaller shapes and added decorations. Which designs are symmetrical? Which designs are nearly symmetrical?

48 *Art for Comfort*
Creating a Fan

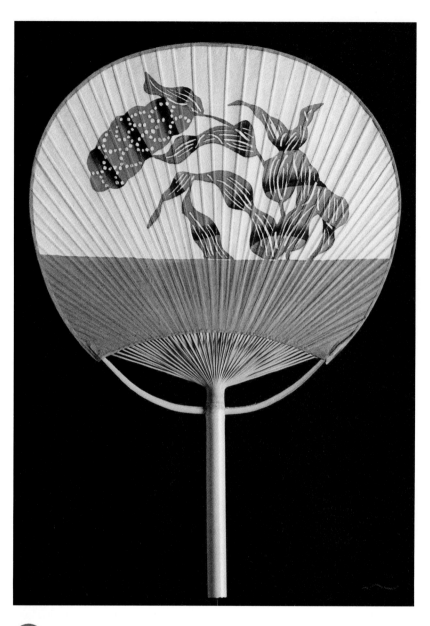

 Keisuka Serizama, *Fan,* Japan, 20th century. Dyed stencil design. Collection of Mingei International.

Useful artworks can be beautiful. For thousands of years people have made useful objects that are beautiful to see.

An artist in Japan created the fan in picture A. The artist was known as a "living treasure." The title "living treasure" is the highest honor for an artist in Japan. It means that people cherish and respect the artist's skill.

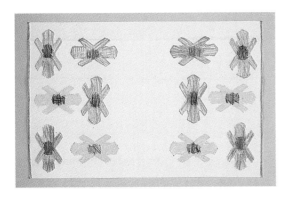

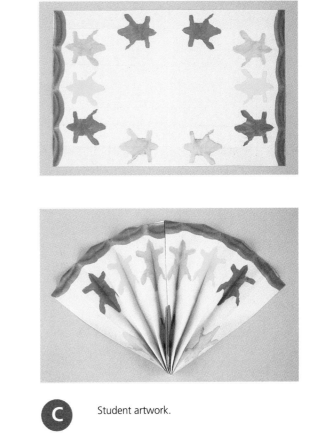

 B Student artwork.

C Student artwork.

Many artists from Japan have a tradition of creating artworks with subtle beauty. **Subtle** means that you must look closely to notice details.

Look again at the fan in picture A. What color scheme did the artist use? What kind of balance do you see in the design? What details give the fan subtle beauty?

Students your age created the fans in pictures B and C. They used related colors. **Related colors** are next to each other on the color wheel. Related colors have subtle similarities and differences.

Create a fan with subtle beauty. Find a related color scheme by looking at the color wheel on page 33. Cut one or several stencils. Print your stencil carefully. When the paint is dry, carefully fan-fold your paper. Then fold the paper in half and tape the center.

Art for Special Times
Making a Mask

 A   **Robert Davidson, *After He Has Seen the Spirit.*** 1980. Wood, paint, feathers, operculum shell, 9 1/2 x 8 1/3 x 4 1/2" (24 x 21 x 12 cm). University of British Columbia Museum of Anthropology (Gift of the Anthropology Shop Volunteers). Photograph: W. McLennan.

 B   ***Rabbit Mask,*** Africa, Mali-Dogon, 19th/20th century. Wood, paint, 5 1/2 x 15 3/4 x 6 3/4" (14 x 40 x 17 cm). The Metropolitan Museum of Art (Gift of Mr. and Mrs. J. Gordon Douglas III, 1982).

People in many cultures create **masks** to keep traditions. Masks are often worn in plays. The masks in pictures A and B help people remember stories about animals and nature.

A Haida Indian artist from Canada created the mask in picture A for a celebration.

The mask has many curved lines. The curves are **symbols** for whales, birds and other animals in Haida stories.

The African mask in picture B shows an imaginary animal who helps farmers. The person who wears the mask dances and pretends to till the soil find pull up weeds. The dance is part of a good luck ceremony.

The masks in pictures A and B help people remember important stories about animals. People in many lands have stories about animals who can speak or act like people. Why do you think stories like this are found in many lands?

Think about stories with animals who act like people. Create a mask of one of your favorite characters. Pictures 1–4 show one way to make a mask.

1. Ask a student to help mark the eyes.

2. Cut out holes for the eyes. What shape do you want them to be?

3. Do you need to trim the sides like this?

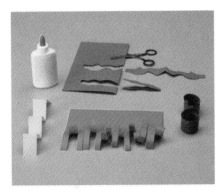

4. How can you add colors and forms to your mask?

 Students created these masks.

117

Some artists use thread, yarn and fabrics for their artwork. These artists are called **fiber artists**. A **fiber** is a long, thin material such as thread or yarn. Can you name some other fibers?

The fabrics in your clothes are made from threads. In some fabrics, the threads go over and under each other. They are woven together.

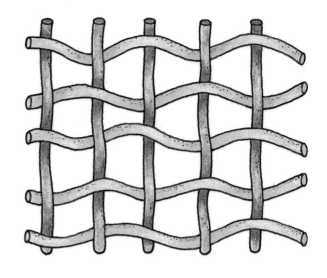

A

Some threads in your clothes are very thick. Some are thin. Are threads different in other ways?

B

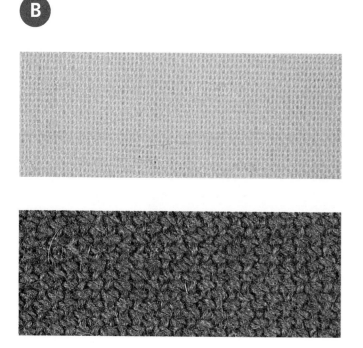

Some fabrics are woven very tightly. The threads are very close together. Some fabrics are woven very loosely. You can see open space between the threads.

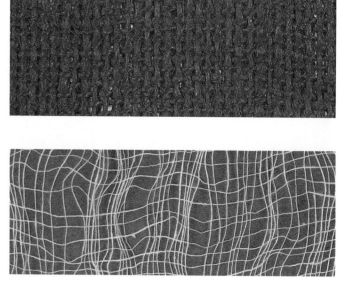

The fiber art in picture C is called **pulled threadwork**. A student created this design in burlap by gently pulling threads out of the cloth. The open spaces create a pattern. Other yarns and stitches also create textures and patterns.

Thousands of years ago, artists in North Africa created clothing with pulled threads. Artists in Europe, Russia and other lands create veils, scarfs or table mats. Some artists create designs for wall hangings.

 Student artwork.

Create your own design in burlap. Gently pull out some threads.

What else can you do to create a new design in the cloth?

Julia Hill, *Africa* (detail), 1985. Silk crepe de chine, resist-painted, 150 x 45" (381 x 114 cm).
Photograph: George Erml.

Do you like to see colorful fabrics? Some artists create dyed fabrics. Dye is a colored liquid that stains the threads in a fabric.

The artwork in picture A is a batik. This **batik** was made by using dyes and wax. The artist brushed warm wax on white cloth. Then she dipped the cloth in dye. The dye resisted, or rolled away from, the areas with wax. She waxed and dyed the cloth many times to create the design.

Student artwork.

B *Adire Eleko Cloth* (detail). Oshogbo, Nigeria, 20th century. Cassava starch, indigo dye. From the collection of Mrs. Cyril Miles.

In Africa, the Yoruba people of Nigeria create batik designs in another way. They apply starch to create designs, then they dye the cloth. This dye is called adire. Adire means indigo, or dark violet, the color of the dye.

You can make a batik design. Make a simple stencil. Your **resist medium** can be a paste-like mixture of hand lotion and toothpaste. Place the stencil on the cloth. Brush this paste-like mixture on the cloth.

When the paste is dry, brush tempera paint over the whole cloth. Then put the cloth under running water. When the paste washes away, you will see a stained design.

121

Linda Benglis, *Patang,* 1980. Satin appliqué on canvas, 15 x 90' (4.5 x 27.4 m).
Atlanta Airport Commission. Photograph: Gary Lee Super.

Some artists create pictures from pieces of cloth or fabric. When the cloth is stitched down, the artwork is called **appliqué**.

Look at the appliqué mural in picture A. The artist used a needle and thread to sew satin fabric on a large piece of canvas. Her abstract design has many shapes based on nature. The shapes seem to dance with a jazzy rhythm.

Unity and variety are important in this design. **Unity** means that all the parts are planned. They look like they belong together. Can you tell how the artist unified the design?

Variety means that parts are different from each other. Variety helps to keep you interested in looking at the work. How has the artist planned for variety?

Student artwork.

Chris Roberts-Antieau, *Shooting Star,* 1989. Fiber appliqué, 24 x 30"
(61 x 76 cm). Courtesy of the artist.

The appliqué in picture B has different kinds of cloth. The stitches are made with a needle and thread or yarn.

The large shapes of the animals fill much of the space. The large shapes help to unify the design. What adds variety to the appliqué?

A student created the appliqué in picture C. You can create your own designs for an appliqué. Collect different kinds of cloth. The textures and patterns in the cloth may give you an idea for a design. Cut out some shapes of cloth. Arrange them on a larger background cloth. Plan your design so it has unity and variety. Then glue the shapes down and add stitches.

53

Sculpture
An Imaginary Animal

A ***Two-Headed Horse***, Early Iron Age, ca. 1000 B.C. Cypriote, terra-cotta, 11 x 5 1/4" (28 x 15 cm). The Metropolitan Museum of Art, New York (The Cesnola Collection).

B ***Two-Headed Serpent,*** 15th century. Aztec. 17 1/2" (44 cm) long. Reproduced by Courtesy of the Trustees of the British Museum, London.

Have you ever seen animals like these? Look carefully. Do these **sculptures** show real or imaginary animals?

The sculpture in picture A is very old. Do the animals look like imaginary horses? Why or why not?

The Mexican sculpture in picture B was made long ago. It is covered with a **mosaic** of tiny shells and colorful stones. The serpent was once a symbol for royalty among the Aztec Indians.

Dragon. Chinese. Rietburg Museum, Zurich, Switzerland. Photograph: Wettstein & Kauf.

The clay dog in picture C looks like a dragon. The sculpture was made in China. It probably shows Fu, an imaginary creature who guards a home with great courage. How did the artist make it look scary?

These are make-believe animals. Find the surprising parts of each sculpture. People in many lands have made sculptures of imaginary animals. Do you know why?

Think of a strange animal that you could make from clay. Make it surprising or scary. Use your imagination!

 Alexander Calder, *The Only, Only Bird,* 1952. Tin and wire, 39 x 18 x 11" (99 x 46 x 28 cm).
© The Phillips Collection, Washington, DC.

Some artists create sculpture from materials they find, such as scraps of wood or metal. The metal rooster in picture A was created by a United States sculptor, Alexander Calder. His artwork is a **found object** sculpture.

Sculpture has form. A **form** has height, width and thickness. Forms are **three-dimensional**. Forms are not flat. What forms did Calder create for his sculpture?

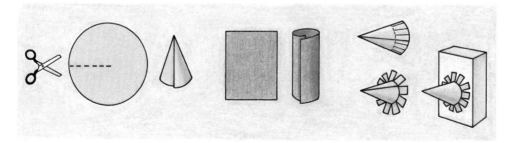

 You can change flat paper into three-dimensional forms.

Robert Hudson, *Charm,* 1964. Polychrome metal sculpture, 45 1/2″ (114 cm). Los Angeles County Museum of Art (Museum Purchase, Contemporary Art Council Funds).

An artist created the sculpture in picture C. He joined many different materials together. Sculpture can be painted, too. What colors and patterns did the artist create?

What can you create from empty boxes, tubes and other materials you find? How can you join the materials together? Can you use your imagination as artists do?

127

Creating a Form
A Sculpture from Paper

 Marvin Finn, *Bird with tall patterned tail.* Painted wood.
Photograph: © Dan Dry.

Sculpture can be made from many materials. The bird in picture A is made from wood. An African-American artist created it.

Where do you see repeated curves? What patterns do you see? What elements unify this work? What elements add variety?

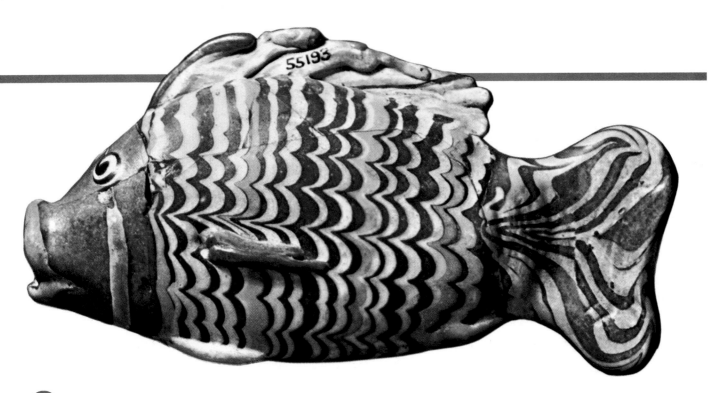

The sculpture in picture B was made in Africa over 3,000 years ago. The form was used as a bottle. The sculpture is unified by the wavy pattern of lines and a simple shape.

Both sculptures are thick shapes. A thick shape is a form. You can create a form from paper. Your form will be a sculpture.

Fold paper. Draw a big, simple shape. Color it.

Cut the folded paper. Color the other side.

Tape some edges. Stuff paper inside. Add tape.

C

D

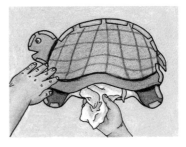

E

129

56

Many artworks have people as a theme. Look at the sculptures in pictures A and D. How are these sculptures of people alike? How are they different? Why do you think many artworks show people?

These sculptures are made from clay. Clay sculptures must be strong. These artists have created thick arms and legs. The clay joints are strong and smooth.

Make a strong sculpture of one person or a group of people. Create the main forms and join them together. Try different positions for the arms, legs and body. Then add details like the nose, ears and mouth.

 William McVey, *Visions.* Stoneware. Wichita Art Association, Inc. Permanent Collection. Purchase Award, Sixth National Decorative Ceramics Exhibition, 1951. Photograph: Mike Fizer. Courtesy of the artist.

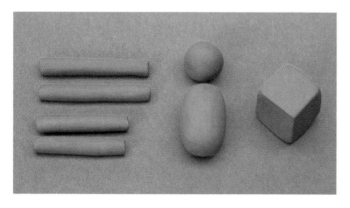

B

C

Three Musicians Seated on a Bench ("Jam Session"), West Mexico, Nayarit, Ixtian del Rio style, about 100 B.C.–A.D. 250. Buff clay with white and red painted decoration, 6 1/2 x 6 1/2 3 1/8" (17 x 17 x 9 cm). Los Angeles County Museum of Art (The Proctor Stafford Collection, Museum Purchase with Balch Funds).

An artist from Mexico created this sculpture. What are the people doing? What makes this clay sculpture strong?

57

Subtracting Clay
A Relief Sculpture

The lively group of musicians in picture A is a carving in wood by African-American artist, Daniel Pressley. The artwork is a relief sculpture. A **relief sculpture** has parts that stand out from a background.

This sculpture is carved from a piece of lumber. The wood is flat and thick. Some shapes stand out from the background. For example, the hands stand out in front of the guitar. Where do you see shapes that stand out?

You can create a relief sculpture. Make a slab of clay. Carve and build up the clay. Create parts that stand up from a background.

B

A Daniel Pressley, *Down By the Riverside,* 1966. Pine relief, 50 x 19" (127 x 48 cm). Schomburg Center for Research in Black Culture, Art & Artifacts Division, The New York Public Library (Astor, Lenox and Tilden Foundations). Photograph: Tom Jenkins.

Winged Deity Relief Sculpture, Assyria, Nimrud, ca. 884–860 B.C. Limestone, 91 1/4 x 71 3/4" (232 x 181 cm). The Nelson-Atkins Museum of Art, Kansas City, Missouri.

D *Giulia Astallia* (Style of L'Antico), ca.1490-1520. Bronze, 2 7/16" (6 cm) diameter. National Gallery of Art, Washington, DC (Samuel H. Kress Collection).

The relief sculpture in picture C was created about 2,800 years ago in Assyria. Assyrian rulers lived in the region of present-day Iran and Iraq.

This sculpture was carved on the walls of an ancient palace. It shows an Assyrian god. He wears a beard and has wings. He is taking care of a palm tree that grows food. This food is still important to people who live in the desert lands of Iran and Iraq.

The relief sculpture in picture D was created about 400 years ago in Italy. It was made to remember a person who died. The writing on the border is the name of the girl.

This relief sculpture is similar to a coin. If you look at a coin, you can see the raised parts and background. You can also close your eyes and feel the relief design.

 Helen Bullard, *Old Mountain Family,* 1970-72. Chestnut slabs, 3 ' 6 1/2" x 18' x 6' 9" (1.1 x 5.5 x 2 m). Photograph: Terry Tomlin.

Helen Bullard carved pieces of very old wood to create the sculpture of a large family in picture A. She wanted to express the idea of many family members living together for a long time. This family lives in the mountains near forests. The wood for the artist's sculpture came from the same forests.

In **carving**, you cut and take away pieces from a solid material like wood or stone. Carving is called a **subtractive** process. If the artist carves very thin parts, they may break off. This is one reason why carving is done slowly and carefully. Each cut is planned first.

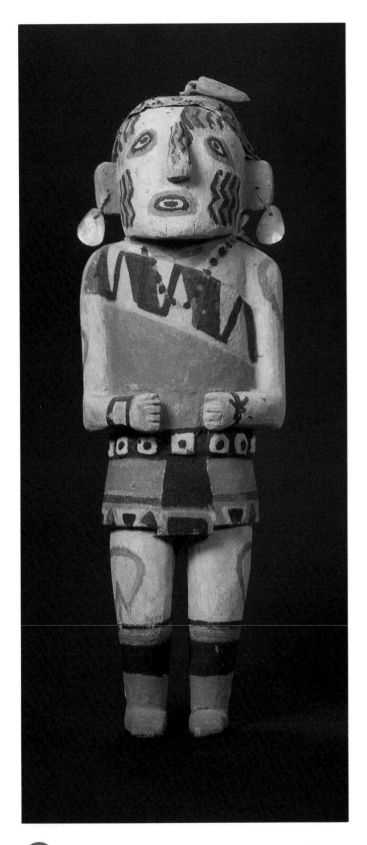

The sculpture in picture B was carved by a North American Indian artist. It is a Kachina doll given to a Hopi child. A Kachina doll is a symbol for a spirit in nature that can teach a lesson. For example, a Kachina doll may have a design that stands for the beauty of flowers or the strength of a bear.

You can practice carving a person. Make a thick **cylinder** of clay. Keep all of the forms close to the body. Plan where you will carve away the clay by drawing guidelines. Carve slowly. Remove just a small amount of clay to show a person.

B **Unknown,** *Hopi Kachina Doll,* ca. 1900. Courtesy of Arrowsmith's, Prescott, Arizona.

C

 Richard Howard Hunt, *Construction,* 1958. Bronze and steel, 20 1/2 x 18 x 12″ (52 x 46 x 30 cm). Hirshhorn Museum and Sculpture Garden, Smithsonian Institution, Washington, DC (Gift of Joseph H. Hirshhorn, 1966).

 Richmond Barthé, *Paul Robeson as Othello*, 1975. Bronze, 20″ (51 cm) tall. Photograph: Armando Solis.

Every person who creates art has special ideas to explore and express. In this lesson, you see sculptures by African-American artists. Each artist works in his or her own way.

Richard Hunt created the sculpture in picture A. He creates many large sculptures for parks and outdoor areas. Richard Hunt says his sculpture combines ideas from nature and from the environment of big cities.

Richmond Barthé created many sculptures about people. He loved the theater and opera. He often created portraits of actors and singers. The portrait in picture B shows a well-known singer of opera.

Betye Saar, *Bittersweet (Bessie Smith Box),* 1974. Assemblage, 14 3/4 x 20 x 2 1/2" (37 x 52 x 6 cm) open. Courtesy of the artist.

The sculpture in picture C is an assemblage by Betye Saar. An assemblage is made from objects or materials the artist finds. This sculpture is inside a box that you can open or close.

Betye Saar likes to collect and save very old objects for her sculpture. Her ideas come from memories of her own life. When she creates a sculpture, she chooses objects that have a similar meaning.

When you look at artworks, you can think about the artists who made them. You can imagine why the artist made them. Why do you think these artists work in different ways?

A Elizabeth Catlett in her studio.

B **Elizabeth Catlett, *Homage to My Young Black Sisters*,** 1969. Cedar, 71 x 14" (180 x 36 cm). Courtesy of the artist.

Elizabeth Catlett, shown in picture A, is a sculptor. She carves wood and stone. She works with metal too.

Elizabeth Catlett made her first carving when she was ten years old. She carved a bar of soap. Her parents thought she should do more artwork. They encouraged her interest in art.

Elizabeth Catlett studied art in college. Later, she became a teacher of art. She creates art in her **studio**, or workplace, at home in Cuernavaca, Mexico. Her husband,

Francisco Mora, is one of Mexico's well-known printmakers.

In picture B, you see two views of a sculpture Elizabeth Catlett carved from wood. Many of her artworks show women and children. Her art expresses the struggles of African Americans for freedom.

Elizabeth Catlett, *Baile (Dance),* 1970. Linocut, 18 x 30" (45 x 76 cm). Courtesy of the artist.

There is one main idea in Elizabeth Catlett's art and in her life. She says that "artists should work for peace, love and equal opportunity for everyone."

Elizabeth Catlett also creates prints. One of her prints is shown in picture C. She creates her prints by carving lines and shapes in blocks of wood or linoleum. This print shows children dancing.

Have you ever seen an artist at work in a studio? An artist's studio has art tools, materials and a place to store artwork.

What kind of art do you like to create? What ideas do you like to express in your artwork?

Judging and Displaying Art

 Erika Wade. Photograph: Christophe Tcheng.

The artists in these two photographs are getting ready for an **art show**. The artist in picture A has selected some of his best work for a show. The artist in picture B is deciding where to hang her sculpture in an **art gallery**.

How do you think these artists choose their work for an art show? Why do you think artists have shows of their works? Have you seen art shows? Where? What kind of art did you see?

 Scott Miles, MFA Student. Courtesy of Savannah College of Art and Design, Georgia.

Your class can have an art show. Everyone will have some artwork in the show. Choose your best artwork. How will you decide which is your best?

Learn to put your best pictures on a mount. A **mount** is a large sheet of paper. Paste your picture on top of the mount so the picture has a border. Follow the steps shown in picture D and listed here.

1. Center the picture on the mount. Be sure the borders are even. Trace around the corners of your picture.

2. Put paste on the back of your picture. Wipe your hands. Then paste the picture down.

3. Make a label for your artwork. Write neatly.

My name is _____.

My work is _____.

It is titled _____.

I learned _____.

D

Art Safety

Study these safety points. Follow other safety points your teacher tells you about.

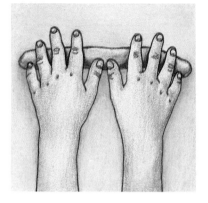

1. If you feel sick or have a health problem, tell your teacher. For example, if you have a rash or scratches on your hands, you should not use clay until your skin heals.

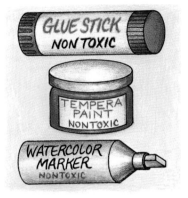

2. Make sure your art materials have a label that says nontoxic. Nontoxic means the materials are safe to use. Read any words that say "Caution." Find out what the words mean.

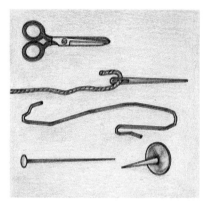

3. Some tools and materials have sharp points or edges. Use these very carefully. Make sure the sharp objects are pointing away from your body.

4. Use all art tools and materials with care. Keep the tools and materials away from your eyes, mouth and face.

5. Learn to use art materials neatly. After art lessons, wash your hands to remove paint, clay or other materials. Always wash your hands before you eat food.

6. If you drop or spill something, quietly help to clean it up. A wet floor or a floor with pieces of art materials on it can be unsafe to walk on.

Ways to Help in Art

Study these examples of ways to help in the artroom. What else can you do to help?

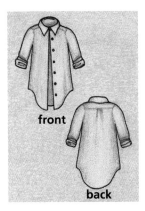

1. Help everyone get ready for art. For some lessons, wear an apron or an old shirt. Button the shirt in the back and roll up the sleeves.

2. Help to clean up. Stack and put art materials away neatly. Wash brushes and store them with the hairs pointing up.

3. Share art tools and materials. Save materials you can use again. You can recycle some materials to create art.

4. Save your artwork in a portfolio. Write your name and the date on all of your sketches and other work. This will help you see and know what you are learning.

5. When you discuss art, listen carefully. Think about what people say. Ask thoughtful questions. In art, there is usually more than one answer to questions.

6. Learn to use art words. Use a dictionary or the glossary on pages 148-154 to find the meaning of art words. Why should you learn art words?

Artists and Artworks

Glossary

angle (ANG-gul). A bend in a line or shape.

animation (an-ah-MAY-shun). Cartoon-like movies with separate pictures drawn by artists. A camera is used to record each picture on a long piece of film or tape. When the film or tape is shown very quickly, you see motion.

appliqué (ah-plee-KAY). Artwork that is made by sewing pieces of cloth onto a cloth background.

arch. A curved or pointed shape in a building; makes an opening in the wall or holds up the roof.

architect (AR-ki-tekt). An artist who designs buildings.

architecture (AR-ki-tek-chur). The art and science of planning buildings and environments for people.

art. A form of visual communication and expression.

art gallery (art GAL-uh-ree). A building, or a space in a building, where artworks are shown.

art media (art MEE-dee-uh). Art materials and their special qualities.

art museum (art myoo-ZEE-um). A building where artwork is shown and carefully saved.

art show. A display of artwork that people are invited to see.

asymmetrical (AY-suh-met-rick-ul). Artwork that looks balanced when the parts are arranged differently on each side.

authentic (ah-THEN-tik). An artwork that is real and not a copy or fake.

balance (BAL-ens). Arrangement in which the parts seem to be equally important or interesting.

batik (bah-TEEK). A process of using wax and dye to make pictures or patterns on cloth.

blend. To mix things together smoothly.

brushstroke. A definite mark or textured area made by using a paintbrush.

canvas (KAN-vus). A strong cloth on which artists create paintings.

carving (KARV-ing). A way to make sculpture by cutting away or subtracting a material such as clay, wood or stone.

center of interest (SEN-ter of IN-trist). The main, or first, thing you notice in an artwork.

ceramics (sir-AM-iks). The art of making objects of fired clay.

city planner (SIT-ee PLAN-er). An artist who helps people design parts of a community or city.

cityscape (SIT-ee-skayp). Artwork that shows a city.

clothing designer (KLOH-thing de-ZI-nuhr). An artist who creates the designs for handmade or manufactured clothing. Often called a fashion designer.

collage (koh-LAHZH). Artwork made by pasting pieces of paper or other materials to a flat surface.

color scheme (KOL-er skeem). A plan for using colors (see **warm colors, cool colors**). The color wheel can help you understand some ways of planning colors.

construct (kon-STRUKT). To create an artwork by putting materials together.

contrast (KON-trast). A great difference between two things. A light color contrasts with a dark color.

cool colors. Colors that remind people of cool things. Varieties of blue, green and violet.

craft. Skill in creating things by hand. Artwork created carefully by hand.

craftsworker. A highly skilled person who creates artwork by hand.

crayon etching (KRAY-on ECH-ing). A process of scratching through one layer of crayon to let another layer of crayon show.

crayon resist (KRAY-on re-ZIST). An artwork created with wax crayons or oil pastels, then covered with watercolor paint. The paint resists, or rolls away from, the wax or oil.

creative (kree-A-tiv). Able to make things in a new or different way.

culture (KUL-chuhr). The special beliefs, customs and way of life of a group of people.

cylinder (SIL-in-dur). A tall round form.

design (de-ZIGN). A plan for arranging the parts or elements of an artwork. An artwork which has a planned arrangement of visual elements.

detail (de-TAYL or DEE-tayl). A small part.

diagonal (di-AG-uh-nul). A line or edge that slants or tilts.

dilute (di-LOOT). Adding a liquid, such as water, to another liquid to make it thinner or flow more easily. A diluted paint flows and lets you blend colors.

distance. (see **perspective**)

dye. A colored liquid that stains the threads in a fabric.

easel (EEZ-uhl). A piece of furniture that is used to hold a painting so it is easy to see and work on.

edge (edj). A line that helps you see a shape, ridge or groove.

elements of design (EL-uh-ments of de-ZIGN). Parts of an artwork that an artist plans, regardless of the subject matter. These elements are line, color, texture, value, space and shape.

enlargement (en-LAHRJ-ment). A picture that has been made larger.

expression (ex-SPRESH-uhn). A special look that communicates a feeling. An expression might be happy, sad, angry or tired.

exterior (ex-STEER-ee-ur). Outside, or the outside of a form.

facade (fah-SAHD). The whole front wall of a main entrance to a building.

fiber (FI-bur). A long, thin material such as thread, yarn or string.

fiber art (FI-bur art). Artwork created from long, thin, thread-like materials.

fiber artist (FI-bur AR-tist). An artist who uses long, thin, thread-like materials to create artwork.

fired (FI-erd). Made hard by great heat (such as a clay object).

form. An element of design. Forms are three-dimensional, such as a cube, sphere or cylinder. They have height, width and thickness. Forms are not flat.

formal design (FOR-mal de-ZIGN). Artwork that has parts arranged the same way on both sides. Also called symmetrical design.

found object (found OB-jekt). Materials that artists find and use for artwork, like scraps of wood, metal or ready-made objects.

geometric (jee-oh-MEH-trik). A shape or form that has smooth, even edges.

graphic designer (GRAF-ik de-ZIGN-er). An artist who plans the lettering and artwork for books, posters and other printed materials.

historical landmark (his-STOR-i-kul LAND-mark). A building or place of importance in history.

horizontal (hor-i-ZON-tal). A straight line that lies flat.

hues (hyooz). The common names for colors, such as red, yellow, blue, orange, green, violet.

illustrate (IL-uh-strayt). The act of drawing a picture to explain something.

illustrator (IL-uh-stray-ter). An artist who creates pictures for books, magazines and the like.

imaginative (ih-MAJ-in-a-tiv). Creating a mental picture of something that is unlike things one has seen.

industrial designer (in-DUS-tree-al de-ZIGN-er). An artist who designs cars, dishes, toys and other products that are made in factories.

informal design (in-FOR-mal de-ZIGN). Artwork that looks balanced when parts are arranged differently on each side. Also called asymmetrical design.

interior (in-TEER-ee-ur). The inner part of something.

interior designer (in-TEER-ee-ur de-ZYN-er). An artist who plans the inner spaces of a building.

intermediate colors (in-ter-MEE-dee-it KOL-ers). Colors that are made from a primary and a secondary color (red-orange, yellow-orange and so on).

kiln (kill). A special oven or furnace that can be heated to a high temperature.

landmark (LAND-mark). Something (a building, a statue, a park) that is easy to see and important to people in a community.

landscape (LAND-skayp). Artwork that shows an outdoor scene.

landscape architect (LAND-skayp AR-ki-tekt). An artists who plans parks, gardens and other outdoor spaces.

line. The path created by a moving point (as one drawn by a pencil point).

mask. An artwork used to cover and disguise a face.

media (see **art media**)

model (MOD-el). A person who poses for an artist. Also, small artwork that shows how a larger artwork might look.

monochromatic (mon-oh-kroh-MAT-ik). A color scheme that uses several values of one color, such as light blue, blue and dark blue.

monoprint (MON-oh-print). A print that is usually limited to one copy.

mosaic (moh-ZAY-ik). Artwork made with small pieces of colored stone, glass or the like.

motion (MOH-shun). Movement, either real or visual.

mount. Paper or cardboard on which a picture is pasted to make a border.

movement (MOOV-ment). Going from one place to another or a feeling of action in an artwork.

mural (MYOOR-uhl). A large painting or artwork, usually designed for a wall.

negative shape or **space** (NEG-eh-tiv shape or space). Shapes or spaces surrounding a line, shape or form.

neutral colors (NEW-tral KOL-ers). In artwork, neutral colors are brown, black, white and gray.

oil paint. A greasy paint that does not mix with water.

original (oh-RIJ-en-al). Artwork that looks very different from other artwork; not copied.

overlap (o-ver-LAP). Overlap means that one shape looks like it is behind another one.

palette (PAL-it). A tray-like surface for mixing colors.

papier-mâché (PA-per MA-shay). A process of making forms by using paper and a diluted paste.

patterns (PAT-terns). Designs that have repeated elements such as lines, colors or shapes.

perspective (pur-SPEK-tiv). Artwork in which the spaces and distances between objects look familiar or "real."

photogram (FOH-toh-gram). A record of shadows that is made on a special photographic paper. The paper is manufactured so that it changes when light strikes the surface.

photograph (foh-TOH-graf). A picture made by using a camera. (see **photography**)

photography (foh-TOG-ruh-fee). The art and science of making a picture by using a camera and film that records the light from a scene.

picture alphabet (PIK-chur AL-fah-bet). In a picture alphabet, the shape of each letter is also a picture.

portrait (POR-trait). Artwork that shows the likeness of a real person.

pose (pohz). A special way to stand or sit.

positive shape or **space** (POZ-ih-tiv shape or space). Shapes or spaces that you see first because they contrast, or stand out from, the background.

primary colors (PRI-meh-ree KOL-ers). Colors from which other colors can be made: red, yellow and blue. (In light, the primary colors are red, green and blue.)

principles of design (PRIN-suh-puhlz of de-ZIGN). Guides for planning relationships among visual elements in artworks. Principles of design are balance, rhythm, proportion, pattern, unity and variety.

prints. Artworks created by pressing sheets of paper on top of an inked design to make copies, or prints, of the design.

product designer (PROD-ukt de-ZYN-er). An artist who plans the appearance of factory-made products, such as cars, furniture, kitchen ware.

proportion (pro-POR-shun). The size, location or amount of something as compared to that of another thing (a hand is about the same length as a face).

pulled threadwork (puld THRED-work). Creating open patterns in cloth by pulling out threads.

radial (RAY-dee-al). Lines or shapes that spread out from a center point.

related colors (ree-LATE-ed KOL-ers). Colors that are next to each other on a color wheel, such as yellow, yellow-green and yellow-orange. Also called analogous colors.

relief sculpture (ree-LEEF SKULP-chur). Sculpture that stands out from a flat background.

repeat (ree-PEET). Using the same design element over and over again to create a pattern.

resist (ree-ZIST). A material, like wax, used to cover or protect a surface from liquids.

Romanesque (roh-man-NESK). An architectural style used for early Christian churches. These buildings have thick walls and small windows with round arches.

rubbing. The process of moving a tool, such as a crayon, across a surface. An artwork made by putting paper over a textured surface and rubbing a crayon on the paper.

scroll (skrohl). A long roll of paper or cloth illustrated with pictures or lettering. Scrolls were used before the invention of books.

sculpture (SKULP-chur). Three-dimensional artwork made by carving, modeling or joining materials.

seascape (SEE-scape). Artwork that shows a scene of the sea or ocean.

secondary colors (sek-on-dayr-ee KOL-ers). Colors that can be mixed from two primary colors; orange, green, violet.

self-portrait (self-POR-tret). A self-portrait is an artwork that shows the likeness of the person who created it.

shade. A color mixed by adding black. A dark value of a hue (dark blue).

shading. Slight or gradual changes in the lightness or darkness of a color or value.

shadow (SHAD-oh). A dark area where there is little light.

shape. The outline, edge or flat surface of a form (a circle or square).

similar designs (SIM-uh-lar de-ZYNZ). Designs that have something in common, but are not exactly alike.

sketch (skech). A drawing that is made to record what you see, explore an idea or to plan another artwork.

space. An empty place or surface, or a three-dimensional area in which something exists.

spirit mask (SPIR-it mask). A mask that is created for use in spiritual ceremonies, not just for fun.

stained glass (staynd glass). Pieces of colored glass that are fitted together like parts of a puzzle, then framed to make a window.

stencil (STEN-sell). A paper or other flat material with a cut-out design that is used for printing. Ink or paint is pressed through the cut-out design onto the surface to be printed.

still life. An artwork that shows non-living things, such as books, candles or the like.

stitchery (STICH-er-ree). Artwork which is made by using a needle and thread or yarn to create stitches on cloth. A stitch is one in-and-out movement of a threaded needle.

storyboard. A set of words and sketches that are made to plan a motion picture or television program. Each sketch shows a scene in the story.

streamlines (STREEM-linz). Graceful, curved lines and edges. The lines look as if they would help something move easily through air or water.

studio (STOO-dee-oh). The place where an artist creates artwork.

style (stile). An artist's special way of creating art. The style of an artwork helps you to know how it is like or different from other artworks.

subtle (SUH-tle). Very slight (to describe changes in color, form, or other visual elements).

subtractive (sub-TRAK-tiv). Cutting or taking away the surface to create the form, as in carving wood.

surface (SUR-fiss). The outermost, or exposed, layer of any form or material.

symbol (SIM-bul). Lines, shapes or colors that have a special meaning. A red heart shape is a symbol for love.

symmetrical (sim-MET-ri-cal). Artwork that looks balanced because parts are arranged in the same way on both sides.

symmetry (SIM-et-ree). Parts arranged the same way on both sides.

technique (tek-NEEK). A special way to create artwork, often by following a special procedure.

tactile (TAK-til). The way something feels when you touch it, such as rough or smooth. (see **texture**)

tempera paint (TEM-per-uh paint). A kind of chalky paint that has water in it. Often called poster paint.

texture (TEKS-chur). The way an object feels when it is touched. Also, the way an object looks like it feels, such as rough or smooth.

three-dimensional (THREE-di-men-chen-al). Artwork that can be measured three ways: height, width, depth (or thickness). Artwork that is not flat.

tint. A light value of a color such as pink. A color mixed with white.

tradition (tra-DISH-en). The handing down of information, beliefs or activities from one generation to another.

transparent (trans-PAR-ent). Possible to see through clearly, such as a clear piece of glass.

two-dimensional (TWO-di-MEN-chen-al). Artwork that is flat and measured in only two ways: height and width.

unity (U-ni-tee). The quality of having all the parts look as if they belong together or work together like a team.

value (VAL-yu). The lightness or darkness of a color (pink is a light value of red).

variety (vah-RI-it-ee). A principle of design. Using different visual elements, such as colors, shapes or lines to create interest in an artwork.

vertical (VUR-ti-kul). Lines that go straight up and down.

viewfinder (VIEW-find-er). A sheet of paper with a hole in it. You look through the hole to "frame" a scene. On a camera, the lens that lets you see what you will photograph.

visual rhythm (VIS-yu-al RITH-um). Visual rhythms are planned by repeating shapes, colors and other visual elements so that they remind you of rhythms in music or dance.

visual symbol (VIS-yu-al SIM-bul). Lines, colors and shapes that stand for something else, as a red heart may stand for love.

warm colors (warm KOL-ers). Colors that remind people of warm things. Varieties of red, yellow and orange.

warm hue. (see **warm colors**)

watercolor paint (WA-ter-KOL-er paint). Special paints that are mixed with water and look like a watery, transparent ink or stain.

weaving (WEEV-ing). Artwork created by locking together separate strands of material (as yarn or thread).

154

Index